Faces™
of the Southern Tier

Portraits and biographies of 50 fascinating subjects.
A reflection of success ~ a celebration of life.

photos by Ed Aswad
editor in chief Roger L. Brooks

J.E.T. Creative Media

265 Main Street, Binghamton, NY 13905 Phone: (800)210-5221

Editor in Chief Roger L. Brooks
Creative Director Elsan Dzudza

Lead Writer Suzanne M. Meredith
Contributing Writer Roger L. Brooks

Lead Editor Tim Mollen
Contributing Editors Roger D. Brooks, Patricia Farrant

Lead Photographer Ed Aswad
Contributing Photographer
   (Behind the Scenes Photos) Roger L. Brooks

Publisher, J.E.T. Creative Media Paul Battisti
Project Coordinator Patricia Farrant

Production Coordinator Elsan Dzudza

First Edition

ISBN 1-891444-10-7

Printed in the United States of America

Written on your face

Today I opened up my eyes
And looked into yours
To see the treasures I could find
That I've never seen before
Cause you possess a story line
And you're longing to be read
And hidden deep within your eyes
Is the life that you have led
(chorus)

Cause there's a way that you speak to me
Without saying a word
And your song owns a melody
That I've never heard
And there's a light in your smile
That's leading the way
And all the dreams that you're chasing
Is written on your face

I see this life in front of me
These stories in a soul
A perfect opportunity
To take the time to know
And appreciate the little things
That make you who you are
Uncover all the mystery
That's hiding in your heart
(chorus)

And every time I see your face
It reminds me of the choice to make
To open up my heart
And listen to the tales you tell
Of all the places that you've dwelled
That make you who you are
Cause I know you've seen a thousand things
And I know you've dreamed a thousand dreams
And this is only the start
To this road of understanding
This knowledge that I'm lacking
This life I hold in regard
(chorus)

©2005 Jared Campbell

Written on your face

by: Jared Campbell

Dedication

To my beautiful daughter, Alexis; whose precious face inspires me to see the beauty in others and gave me inspiration for this book.

Acknowledgements

This project was the labor of many. Heartfelt thanks to Ed Aswad and Sue Meredith who believed in it from the start; to Elsan Dzudza and Tricia Farrant who worked so very hard on this project; to Tim Mollen for his speedy and efficient work; to Jared Campbell for his superb writing abilities in the song he wrote for the DVD and website; to Nestle´and Emily Raimondi for their photo-shoot assistance; to my parents, Roger and Nancy Brooks, who are always there for support; to all my friends and family who offered advice and encouragement; and, finally, to my wife, Sabrina. Without her love and understanding this would not have been possible. -Roger L. Brooks

Contents

faces

Introduction

Why *FACES*?

Too often, we go through life without taking the time to see people for who they really are. We are so busy and caught up in our own worlds that we seldom take time to pay tribute to our neighbors. Yes, I admit, I'm part of this rat race. Only when my newborn daughter was diagnosed with a deformity called a hemangioma did I start to see the beauty of others around me. It was very painful for my wife and me to witness what initially seemed to be a scratch on our two week-old daughter's eyelid and brow grow into a large, aggressive, and thankfully benign lesion. She was our firstborn, and we didn't even have time to enjoy our new creation. Instead, we spent the next full year seeking out doctors around the country who could treat her disorder.

Luckily, we found the sole doctor in the country that specializes in treating hemangioma lesions. His name is Dr. Milton Waner, and he had just transferred to New York City from the University of Arkansas Children's Hospital. We felt a great deal of relief when his first words after hello were, "I can fix this." That was undoubtedly the happiest day of my life. He told us that after one or two surgeries our daughter would look normal. He didn't want to wait, and immediately scheduled surgery. What did this mean for my wife and me? No more intrusive questions from people, no more strange looks, and no more doctor visits. He said it would take about a year to complete the treatment, but in the big picture, a year was no time at all.

The surgeries went very smoothly and our daughter looked better with each passing week. But there was one problem that kept weighing on my mind. What about all the other children that were as badly disfigured or more so than our daughter? What would happen to them? There are infants and toddlers with large growths on their faces. Some have multiple growths affecting the eyes, nose, lips, ears, neck and skull. What would their prognosis be? I felt some relief that they were in the same waiting room as us, waiting to see the same miracle doctor, but this experience really put the human face into perspective for me. A face is not just a face. A face is the most precious part of our visible person, and no face should ever be taken for granted.

Creation of the Book

After a few sleepless nights, I came up with a concept of how to dedicate a part of my life to recognizing others. I wanted to compile a book full of people from all walks of life. I wanted to recognize them, tell their stories, and more importantly, photograph their faces. I couldn't think of a more appropriate name for the book than *FACES*. I put a talented team together, and six months later we have our first published edition. When I met with award-winning photographer Ed Aswad and told him about the concept for the book, he understood immediately what I was hoping to accomplish. His initial reaction was, "the lines on people's faces tell their life story." That statement rings true. Each decision we make, each time we make a mistake, and each smile we take is recorded on our face. Ed's words really hit home for me, and I was excited when Ed agreed to join the team. We were off to a good start.

FACES is a reflection of success and a celebration of life. It's a book honoring ordinary people with extraordinary talents, abilities, or resolve. Too often, people are not acknowledged for who they are, or for the talents they share. You'll notice that this book is made up of subjects from all walks of life. There are some individuals you may recognize, and others you may not. The mission was to seek out people who play important roles in the life of our community. Whether or not the person is well-known had no impact on the selections. I'm a firm believer that we all have the opportunity to do good, but it's those who make a commitment to live their lives in a positive way who really shine.

Some people are born with more natural talent than others, and there are others who find their talent or niche and develop it into something special. Whatever abilities, talents, or needs we have, we are all here in this world with our own role to play. But it is up to each individual to define that role and cultivate it. There are people with very specific and noticeable talents, and others that simply go about life in their own way, yet make a sizable contribution through what they do. This book honors a collection of people based on who they are and what they do to make a difference in the world we live in today.

faces

Criteria

The Southern Tier has a pool of very talented people living here. How did we go about choosing this group? Who are they, and what is their outlook on the roles that they play? There are so many fascinating people that we ordinarily wouldn't have a chance to learn about. My objective was to seek out those people and let their stories be told. Our team went out and canvassed the area to find fifty of the most interesting subjects we could find. We could have easily selected several hundred subjects. But we narrowed the number down to make this book manageable in its scope and appealing in its design. Our goal is to select and publish fifty new subjects each year in a new edition of *FACES*.

The criterion for consideration is as follows:
The subject must be a living resident of the Southern Tier.
The subject must have a special talent, ability or resolve in what they do.
The subject must touch the lives of others in a positive way.

It was difficult to narrow our initial list down to fifty subjects who met these three criteria. Beginning next year, we will open nominations up to the general public, who will be able to vote for their choice of who should appear in the next edition. All nominations will be considered, and the names of those nominated will remain on our list for up to three years, or until that person is selected.

There may be choices for this book that some would disagree with. That is why it is important for readers to know that there are no specific rules for entry. Whether we like someone or not is certainly not a criterion for entry. It's not up to any one individual to judge if someone is *worthy*. We'll leave the judging to a higher power. Remember, this book is a celebration of people – not a popularity contest, not a *Who's Who* of the Southern Tier, and not a platform for personal gain. There are no fees to participate. There are no catches. If a person is recommended, the *FACES* staff will perform our due-diligence, and then make a decision on the subject's entry.

Touching Success

We all know life is not easy. We're taught from a young age that success is the greatest achievement we can strive for in life. It certainly can be; however, how we define success can be as diverse as individuals themselves. I have found that success has two common denominators. Surrounding one's self with intelligent, hardworking people, and following through on whatever your mission is. In talking with the subjects of this book, people overwhelmingly attributed success to either their upbringing, or to an inner-resolve or burning desire to succeed. In many ways, the comforts of today have diluted the burning need to strive toward specific goals. The continuing development of technology, however, has allowed people to reach for their goals in a more swift, reliable, and accurate way. The fact is, there will always be debate on why or how certain individuals succeed versus others. Is it resources, access, or even luck?

If a study was performed on the individuals in this book, there would most likely be some common reasons for their individual successes. Our goal, however, is not to conduct a study. We simply want to bring into focus fifty faces. They are young, old, and in between. Our definition of success has no specific formula, either. We all have our own definitions, explanations, classifications, and descriptions of how we perceive success, but the fact of the matter is in today's world one can be deemed successful by simply surviving and providing the bare necessities for ourselves and our families. We sought out those who stand out above their peers, and persevere in their respected fields.

History

The second element that inspired me to pursue this project was the value of local history. I want our children, grandchildren and great-grandchildren to open *FACES* in ten, fifty, or even a hundred years to see some of the faces of our time. Think of all the many faces that we've encountered that we'll never know anything about. Think of all the individual success stories that have helped mold our community into what it is today. There were so many gifted people that were either born or settled here before us that we know very little to nothing about. From doctors to tradesmen, and public servants to schoolteachers, there are so many men and women that will never be known for all the positive contributions they've made. We can make a difference going forward, however, by telling the stories of those who make a difference in our world today.

-Roger L. Brooks

faces

01 Alex Alexander

founder, b.c. open

"When a person has a vision of what is possible, it is the Lord telling them something. Then it is time to really make changes. People can do anything if they believe." Those are the words of Alex Alexander.

Alex is the epitome of a good man with a good idea. That idea turned into one of the biggest success stories in the Southern Tier. Known as the "father of the B.C. Open," Alex was born and raised in Endicott and his devotion to his hometown has never wavered. He has put a lifetime of effort into the PGA golf tournament and the Broome Community Charities organization.

Starting the B.C. Open in 1971 is only one of the dramatic ways Alex has made life better for everyone in Broome County. He raised the money to build the Endicott Boys and Girls Club, served on the Broome County Arena Board, raised funds for the Endicott Visitor Center, and helped make it possible to build the Greek Orthodox Church of the Annunciation in Vestal, NY. During all this activity, he continued to operate Alexander Harvey Clothing, have a home with a great wife and children, and participate and lead in the Endicott Rotary Club. He aided the county in building the Grippen Park Ice Skating rink and acquiring Round Top Park.

Although Alex did not plan on such a long-term association with the B.C. Open, he persevered and became both the oldest and longest-serving chairman of a PGA event. According to him, he just did his best, one year at a time. "Action, in my book, is more meaningful than words. Get the job done. If it is for the benefit of others no task is too great."

Did You Know:

In 1984, Governor Mario Cuomo presented Alex with the New York Regents Medal for community service.

01

Alex **Alexander**

faces

02 | *Senator Warren Anderson*

senator

Warren M. Anderson is a partner of Hinman, Howard & Kattell, LLP in Binghamton. However, he is best known for his service as a New York State Senator from 1953 through 1988. From 1973 until 1988, he was the Temporary President and Majority Leader of the State Senate. In these powerful positions, Anderson represented the interests of all the people of New York. Residents of the Southern Tier can also thank him for the building of Interstate 88 to Albany. "I spent a lot of time on that road, contemplating strategies for the Senate," says Anderson.

By the time Senator Anderson reached college, he knew law and politics were in his future. He enjoyed being an attorney, and working in the government law center of Albany was made easier because of his extensive law background.

Of his days in the State Senate, he says, "I made many life-long friends while serving in the Senate, and serving is the operative word. I always tried to guide with humor, as well as being prepared with information." Senator Anderson's numerous civic activities include serving as the Vice Chairman of the Board of Trustees of the New York State Historical Association, and as a member of the Advisory Committee at the Government Law Center at Albany Law School. He is also a member of the New York State Commission on Judicial Nomination, the Hartwick College Council, and the Board of Overseers of the Nelson A. Rockefeller Institute of Government.

After his Senate career, Senator Anderson remained here in the Southern Tier. As he explains, "This is a fine area in which to live, and I am now enjoying more family life – and golf! I never wanted to live anywhere else."

But his mind is never far from good governance. Here's his take on the future: "I believe the government will be fair. There will always be Social Security, but with some revisions. The economic environment is certainly improving, with a lot of diverse commerce. My advice to future generations is to 'love thy neighbor.' You do not need much more than that for a law."

Did You Know: Senator Anderson played a round of golf in Augusta, Ga. with Congressman Amo Houghton, in which he shot par on all three par-three holes.

02

Warren Anderson

Fran Angeline

coach

"If you give everything you've got, every minute, then some good things have to come your way." Putting those words into practice, Fran Angeline has set a precedent for excellence in the sports of football and tennis, as well as in his contribution to his community.

Fran is a native of Endicott who chose to remain in his hometown – teaching, coaching, and winning. At one time, he was considered one of the top tennis players in the Southern Tier. He earned the title of "Mr. Tennis" for his top-notch playing and his promotion of the sport. He was instrumental in the construction of tennis facilities at Union-Endicott High School and in the Village of Endicott.

Fran is perhaps best known for his record as the most winning high school coach in the area. Football is where he made his mark on thousands of fans and players. Fran won countless accolades as the football coach of Union-Endicott High School, producing All Star and All State players. In 1964, he led UE to its first championship in the history of the school. The grateful school community named the UE field house after him.

Fran was chosen to be in the Who's Who in National Athletics, and was named New York State Coach of the Year by the New York State Sports Writers Association. He was also named Coach of the Year by the High School Football Coaches of America.

Community service is also an important part of Fran's life. He works with the Broome-Tioga Special Olympics, the Endicott Rotary Club, and many other non-profit organizations.

Fran sums up his personal philosophy this way: "You may never get the opportunity to do your best again, because you only pass through once."

Did You Know:
Fran organizes and participates in a group of Christmas carolers called the Tiger Elites.

03

Fran Angeline

The event of life is always with Fran.

motivators

One recurring theme in the lives of Francis and Helen Battisti is an attitude of caring and sharing. Francis L. Battisti, LCSW, DCD is the CEO of the Battisti Network, a multi-discipline consulting firm specializing in individual and organizational transformations. He is a Professor of Psychology and Human Services at Broome Community College. Francis is also a practicing psychotherapist, specializing in work with aging individuals and families. He has a national reputation in the field of conflict disposition, and his workshops have been offered throughout the U.S., Canada, and the Caribbean. He has impressive credentials as a seminar presenter and keynote speaker. He does all this while serving on numerous boards of directors, and authoring several videos and audiotapes. His new book is entitled *Checchino: A Father Son Journey Toward Dusk*, and he and Helen co-authored the book *Tomorrow's Weight...The No-Diet Way to Lose Weight*.

Helen E. Battisti is also an exceptionally accomplished and involved person. She is the CNO of the Battisti Network, and an adjunct professor at Marywood University and BCC. Using her M.S. degree in Foods and Nutrition, she is a registered dietitian. She balances her home, volunteer and professional lives with an energy deeply based on the need to share her talents. She is currently a candidate for a Ph.D. in Human Development.

These talented people have been married to each other for thirty years and are the parents of three sons. Helen comments, "We are devoted to our family and to giving back to the community. We want to make things better for the human situation. We have a great deal of faith. If a person does not have faith, they have no conscience. We hope to encourage the young to expand their ideas and be creative thinkers. Yesterday's solutions will not answer today's problems."

Francis is in agreement, and he adds, "We have an obligation to the future. We often use running as a metaphor for life. People need to keep their minds moving into new ways to think and create. We need to listen to the wisdom of the older generations and use it for modern solutions...joining together to stop the legacy of selfishness in the community, the country, and the world. If our work has positively encouraged others to grow and learn, then their accomplishments are our legacy."

Did You Know:
Fran and Helen were on the medical staff at Woodstock 2 in 1994.

04

Battisti

Ron Benjamin

attorney

"The primary reason I do a fair amount of civil rights cases is that I feel what comes around goes around. I was fortunate to have many conscientious people help me when I was in need and I'm trying to do the same", says Ronald Benjamin.

A graduate of Buffalo Law School, Benjamin saw inequities in the legal system firsthand in 1971, as the Executive Director of PROBE, a prisoner rehabilitation program in Binghamton. Believing the system fails those who needed help the most, he opened his law firm in 1979 to concentrate on public interest law. He soon gained a reputation as a "brash young attorney." Today, he makes it clear that his passion for public interest law has not mellowed. His successful experiences in civil rights litigation have made him a powerful advocate for individuals in need of representation.

Ron Benjamin's firm seeks redress for a wide range of wrongdoings, including product liability and personal injury. He has a hardball litigation style in dealing with government entities and large corporations. In 1991, he secured the highest individual jury verdict in the history of the United States on behalf of clients who sustained injury from the use of a prescription drug.

Ron states, "Although practical realities have resulted in our moving into other areas of law, with an emphasis on suing pharmaceutical companies who place dangerous drugs in the marketplace, we remain very active in civil rights litigation ranging from representing disadvantaged and handicapped children to misconduct by police. We remain committed to both the public interest and the individual interests of our clients and have the significant trial experience necessary to realize a maximum recovery on behalf of our clients."

Ron Benjamin says that he always searches for the deeper truth behind corporate and municipal policies that make life unfair for the uninformed and the poor. He plans to continue striving for legal changes to help communities and individuals. Although he grew up in Manhattan, he continues to choose this area to live and raise a family, believing this community is the best environment for a safe and wholesome atmosphere.

Did You Know:
Ron Benjamin has a keen interest in American history, and especially the American Revolutionary War.

05

Ron Benjamin

Tony Brunelli

photorealist

If you have a chance to meet Anthony Brunelli and talk to him in person about the ongoing revitalization of Binghamton, you will catch some of his contagious enthusiasm. When it comes to discussing and working toward the current and future growth of Binghamton's city center, no one is more intense or accomplished.

Brunelli is a professional artist at the pinnacle of national and international recognition for his photorealist paintings. Brunelli's paintings can easily be mistaken for photographs. His talent allows him to capture the most amazing details from a photograph, and display those details in lush paint strokes. Brunelli began his journey as an artist with studies at Broome Community College, the Columbus College of Art Design, and Binghamton University, where he earned his Bachelor of Arts. Then, in 1992, he walked into the Meisel Art Gallery in Manhattan. Louis Meisel, the proprietor of the gallery, immediately liked what he saw in Brunelli's style of realism. He went on to sell many of Brunelli's works, and he continues to represent the artist today.

Many of Brunelli's early paintings captured evocative images of downtown Binghamton, and brought those images to audiences around the globe. He has since been commissioned by collectors worldwide to capture scenes in the Binghamton area and in locations as far away as Vietnam, Paris and Prague. His paintings have been exhibited since 1989, and in 2004-2005, his work was displayed as part of the American Photorealism Traveling Exhibition in Japan, Italy and the United States.

Partly through his leadership, a thriving art colony has been established in downtown Binghamton, anchored by his Brunelli Fine Arts Gallery, which opened in 2003. Brunelli purchased and completely renovated the vintage brick building, designing the two bottom floors for his gallery, the two middle floors for his home, and the top floor for his studio. The gallery has hosted an array of upcoming and well-known artists, photographers, and sculptors. The Brunelli Fine Arts Gallery provides a venue, a hub, and a heart for the Binghamton arts community.

Anthony Brunelli fulfilled his childhood dream of owning and renovating an old building with character, and he continues to choose to live and work in Binghamton. His efforts are inspiring, and his enthusiasm is spreading, as thousands of people each month are able to appreciate art in so many different forms. His works of art and his revitalization efforts will continue to make Binghamton a better and more beautiful place to live.

Did You Know:
Anthony Brunelli enjoys cooking. His specialty is a Vietnamese soup dish called pho.

06

Tony Brunelli

Jared Campbell

singer/songwriter

In the two short years he has been pursuing his music career, Jared Campbell, a 23 year-old singer-songwriter from Binghamton, has established himself as a fixture in the Northeast's independent music scene. By connecting with his audience on a personal level, Jared has not only built a loyal fan base, but has sold over 10,000 CDs – a major accomplishment for an independent artist.

Jared has achieved a number of notable career milestones. He was chosen by MTV Books to record a track for their short story collection Lit Riffs. He has shared the concert stage with national acts such as Jason Mraz, Gavin DeGraw, Journey, Matt Nathanson, Sister Hazel, and more. The celebration concert for the release of his first full-length CD, *Rest Out*, sold out Binghamton's 1,500-seat Forum Theater. This was an important achievement for Jared, because he had attended many concerts at this venue while he was growing up, dreaming that someday he would be the one onstage.

As Jared explains, his goal "is to have my music impact the lives of my listeners." He does this with feel-good songs like *Only Getting Better*, and with deeply rooted songs like *Catch A Glimpse of Blue*, which is about overcoming life's obstacles. Although Jared's CDs are recorded with a full band, he typically performs live as a solo acoustic artist. This affords him the opportunity to invite listeners into the depth of his songs. His debut EP, *Where It All Begins*, only hints at the depth of his songwriting ability, inviting listeners to not only discover who Jared is as a person, but to reflect on their own lives. *Rest Out* highlights Jared's growth as a musician and takes his songs to another level – one that builds upon Jared's continuing goal of not only providing entertainment but also provoking thought.

Jared's fans will be anxiously watching to see what's in Jared's future *House of Cards* – which can only add to his already impressive list of accomplishments.

Did You Know:
Jared won a contest and trip to *Saturday Night Live* in NYC for doing an exceptional impression of Chris Farley.

07

Jared Campbell

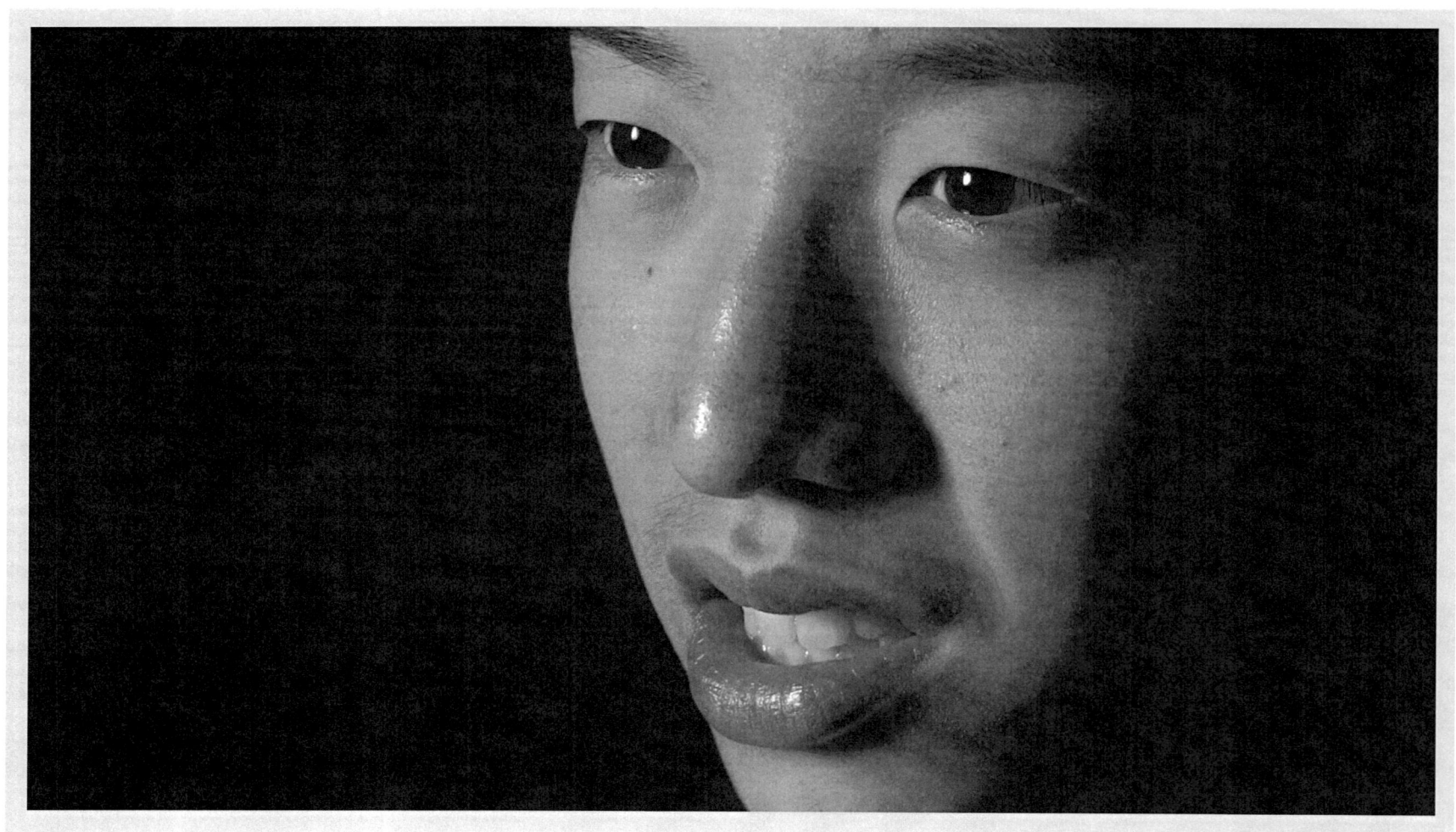

whiz kid

Twenty years ago, Zu-yan Chen and Hong Zhang married and emigrated from mainland China to the United States. Their children Eric and Angela were born in this country. Eric Chen credits his parents with giving him a driving ambition to succeed, and at 17 years of age, he has already been achieving distinction. For example, last year Eric received a perfect score of 2400 on the SAT exams.

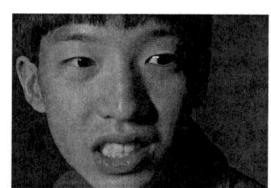

Eric has earned several awards at state and local math and science competitions, including a gold medal at the State Science Olympiad competition. In 2001-2002, he was the New York State Spelling Bee Champion. These are only part of his accomplishments, as he has participated in a well-rounded complement of activities. In sports, Eric plays varsity tennis on the Vestal High School team and enjoys playing table tennis with his father and friends in local tournaments.

Music is another important element in Eric's life. He enjoys playing the piano, and his playing earned him second place in the Endicott Performing Arts Center Talent Competition. He also plays percussion, and won second place in the Southern Tier Music Teacher's Association High School Competition for a timpani solo.

As if this were not enough to keep the high school senior busy, Eric also is Vice President of Tutoring for Vestal's chapter of the National Honor Society, President of the Mathletes, and President of the Science Club. He also volunteers his time at the Discovery Center of the Southern Tier.

Happily, Eric still enjoys being a kid. "I believe in working hard, but also in saving some time to relax and enjoy friends and to have a little fun. I think this is the recipe for success."

Did You Know:
Eric is one of the two boys at Vestal High School who started the Ping Pong Club.

08

Eric **Chen**

Ryan Connolly

athlete

Ryan Michael Connolly is the only son of Penny and the late Michael Connolly. Ryan has always been a stellar athlete, excelling in baseball and football at Binghamton High School and in hockey with the Binghamton Junior Senators. Based on his high batting average, Ryan was ranked the #12 high school baseball prospect in New York State. In addition to being a superb athlete, Ryan also excels in academics. Upon his graduation in 2005, he received an International Baccalaureate Diploma. In addition, Ryan was active in various clubs and organizations at Binghamton High, such as Binghamton Athletes Care, a program where student-athletes visit elementary schools to talk to children about positive decision making. He was also part of Students Against Drunk Driving, the National Honor Society, Patriots Putting a Stop on Smoking, the Varsity B Club, and the Iron Blood weightlifting program. Because of his achievements, Ryan was selected for inclusion in *Who's Who Among American High School Students*.

On November 10, 2004, Ryan signed a letter of intent to play baseball for the University of Notre Dame on a full athletic scholarship. His defensive skills as a catcher and his excellent batting average helped earn his scholarship with the Fighting Irish. Ryan says, "The biggest thing that marks my life so far, other than being at Notre Dame, is the loss of my father. When I was thirteen, he was diagnosed with lung cancer. Nearly two years later, he passed away at the age of thirty-nine. This has been the most difficult time in my life. Since then, one of the biggest projects that my mother and I have taken on is the foundation that we have set up in his name."

In the spring of 2005, Ryan and Penny Connolly established The Michael E. Connolly Endowment for Lung Cancer Research. The mother-son team has an immediate goal to raise $500,000, but Ryan explains, "We are really reaching for the million-dollar mark, and at this point we feel extremely confident that we will do so. This is something that is going to keep my father's name alive forever." Knowing Ryan's skill-set and determination, it's a goal the duo will most certainly reach.

Did You Know:
Ryan hit a home run in the American Legion World Youth Classic for Post 1645 at the age of 13.

09

Ryan **Connolly**

Nate Cortese

restauranteur

The name Cortese is synonymous with pizza. When the restaurant opened in the late 1940's many people were not familiar with pizza; it was often known as "hot pie". So, Nate Cortese began passing out samples, and soon they could not keep up with the demand for the "pies." Today, people near and far who have had the opportunity to taste a Cortese pizza often return – even if just passing through town.

For 58 years, Cortese Restaurant continues serving culinary delights to the public. From the beginning, Nate has been an integral part of the business.

The Cortese family came to Binghamton in 1928, when Nate was just six years old. By age 13, he was working in a local restaurant to help the family survive the Great Depression. In 1942, Nate and his two brothers were part of the United States military, serving their country during World War II. This put the family dream of owning a restaurant on hold until 1947, when Nate's father Corrado purchased a suitable building. Unfortunately, only two of the brothers returned from the war. Angelo Cortese was killed in action on Mindoro Island in the Philippines. Nate says the family's profound faith convinced them that Angelo was with them in spirit as Cortese Restaurant opened its doors in October of 1947. Total sales for the first day of business were equal to half a case of beer.

Nate has served on the New York State Restaurant Association Board of Directors, on the Board of Directors for Mom's House, and on the Board of Trustees for Birthright of Binghamton. He is also a Fourth Degree member of the Knights of Columbus. One of his favorite sayings is, "A good reputation is priceless. It cannot be bought - it must be earned."

An early entrepreneur and believer in the value of the Broome County area, Nate is a modest person, giving credit for his success to his wife Joan, to their family, and to God.

Did You Know: As a youngster, Nate broke a window of a restauranteur and went to work to pay for the window. That was his entrée into the restaurant world.

10

Nate Cortese

Kristine Cunningham

community servant

"I think that service to the community is a necessity if we want to build a strong and healthy future. By sharing our talents, we can have such a positive impact on others, and I truly feel that we will be blessed in return," says Kristine Cunningham. Kristine has shared her talents, and what started out as an internship quickly turned into a career. For the past twelve years, Kristine participated in offering hope and opportunity to young parents striving for a better future at the non-profit agency Mom's House.

When Kristine graduated from Binghamton University, she was looking for an internship position in her field of social work. She secured a position at Mom's House, and after some time, she says everything "just clicked." She eventually took over as Executive Director, falling into something she learned to care so much about. "I really got to love the program over the years," she says. "What I thought was a stepping stone position turned into a career."

The philosophy of Mom's House is to support single parents in their quest to make a better life for themselves and their children. The parents and children she helped were Kristine's personal inspiration for achieving her own goals of making Mom's House secure for future generations. She encouraged others to believe any worthy aspirations were not beyond reach. A beautiful new facility in Johnson City was the result. A capital campaign program conducted over two years of intensive coordination raised $550,000 to make the building possible.

Kristine went on to receive a MS degree from Binghamton University in Business Administration. She says she applied her studies to her career at Mom's House. Now a mother herself, she remains a volunteer for Mom's House – something she says she'll always do. "I will always volunteer my time and monetarily support the program." Kristine sums up her goals for life this way: "I hope that at the end of my life I can look back and say that I provided a positive, nurturing, and loving environment for my children and that I had some sort of positive impact on my community."

Did You Know:
Kristine has a large collection of beer bottles and cans that her father brought back to her from all over the world.

11

Kristine Cunningham

Dr. Lois DeFleur

b.u. president

Since 1990, Dr. Lois B. DeFleur has been leading Binghamton University as its fifth president. This latest phase in her career builds on her previous experience as an eminent sociologist and college administrator.

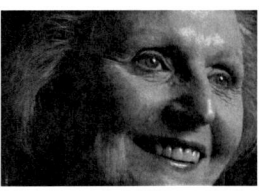

Binghamton University has more than 14,000 undergraduate and graduate students. Dr. DeFleur guides the University's liberal arts programs in Harpur College, in addition to four professional schools, and a number of associated masters and doctoral programs. Since she took office, she has led the University through a period of funding challenges, while enhancing planning processes and developing innovative programs.

During Dr. DeFleur's tenure, the University has constructed two major academic buildings, doubled the size of its University Union, added several residence halls and one new residence community and completed a $33.1 million Events Center to help showcase its Division I athletics program. An additional and exciting project is planned which will consist of the construction of a Downtown Education and Community Development Center in the city of Binghamton.

President DeFleur has significantly enhanced University relationships with external groups. Since her arrival at Binghamton, the University's endowment has risen from approximately $8 million to $51 million and faculty research awards have increased 60 percent.

Dr. DeFleur came to Binghamton from the University of Missouri-Columbia where she had been provost. Dozens of boards of directors have benefited from her participation, including the National Association of State Universities and Land-Grant Colleges, and the American Council on Education, as well as many non-profit and corporate boards. For her ongoing dedication, she was presented with the Civic Leadership Award from the Greater Binghamton Chamber of Commerce, as well as dozens of awards from other organizations.

Did You Know:
President DeFleur is a pilot and the owner of a Comanche 260, which she has flown for more than three decades.

12

Lois DeFleur

Rev. Gary Doupe

reverend

The Reverend Gary E. Doupe's inspiration in life was gained from people who care deeply about others, including the Reverend Dr. Martin Luther King. It was Dr. King's words that motivated Gary to spend his life seeking justice for all people.

The common threads that run through the life of Reverend Doupe are faith and peace. Born in Bainbridge, NY, he attended public schools in Vestal and then received a B.A. degree from Binghamton University. He received a Master of Divinity degree from Wesley Theological Seminary in Washington, D.C., and went on earn a Doctorate of Ministry from the San Francisco Theological Seminary in San Anselmo, California.

Pastor Doupe served several churches in the Wyoming Conference before his retirement in 2005. Throughout the years, he and his wife Elaine raised their family and maintained an interest in the community in addition to their church activities. Wherever he served, the congregations were encouraged to be inclusive and mindful of human rights. The Doupes chose to remain in the Southern Tier of New York because, "This area is geographically blessed with two beautiful rivers and some of the most bucolic countryside to be found in the world. It contains creative people who pursue a wide variety of artistic and humane projects, making this a healthy, productive place to live."

Along with his pastoral duties, Gary was involved with Habitat for Humanity and calling people together through music and theatre productions. As he puts it, "I believe music is a universal and divine gift that can reach into the soul and touch the best in each of us."

Gary sums up his philosophy this way: "If I can pass along what other people have given me out of generosity and care – the basis of the Golden Rule – then I will be satisfied. Every ounce of energy invested in other people comes back multiplied as blessings. I hope I have encouraged others to discover this joy."

Did You Know:
In 1969, Gary was ordained an Elder at the Wyoming Annual Conference of the United Methodist Church.

13

Gary **Doupe**

faces

Ed Folli

coach

"I'm really driven to be the very best in whatever I do. I think I have to be. I have this drive inside of me - be it for teaching, coaching or the starter on the golf course". Those are quite powerful words from one of the most powerful mindsets of our era. Ed Folli has been an intense presence for his students and student-athletes at Union-Endicott High School for over thirty years. He has been the varsity baseball coach sine 1990.

Referring to baseball as the most cerebral game in sports, Ed Folli (nickname Folls) is a student of the game, and says he continues to learn more each day. He keeps a notepad with him as he watches his favorite team, the NY Mets, or any game that may be on television. He says his late father, Ateo, is perhaps the biggest reason this "little guy" overcame any obstacle in his path to succeed. Folls explains, "My dad, God rest his soul, used to tell me – 'just because you're small doesn't mean you're not good.' Those words really inspired me. I was only 147 pounds in high school, so I used his encouragement to excel in sports, as a player and as a coach."

He credits former UE Football Coach Fran Angeline (see pg. 6) as his mentor. "Outside of my father, he influenced my life more than any other person," says Folls. He also gives a world of credit to his best friend and college roommate, Barry Weinberg. Barry became head athletic trainer of the St. Louis Cardinals in 1998, after 16 seasons with the Oakland Athletics. Folls says, "My very good friend allowed me an avenue to the big leagues that most people don't have. Being able to converse with professionals like Tony LaRussa has certainly elevated my strategies." This access also played a role for his own kids, as they accompanied dad to the Bigs on many occasions.

Folls and his wife Wendi have two sets of twins, and they are all athletes. Folls' love for sports has certainly been instilled in his children. Michael and E.J., the elder set of twins, are excelling in college athletics, while Meagan and Ty continue to stand out at UE High School. A 1969 graduate of UE, this lifelong resident of Endicott graduated from Springfield College in MA, where he was selected to the All New England Baseball Team in 1973. He succeeded his role model Pete Sylvester in the post of Varsity Baseball Coach in 1990. His Tiger teams have enjoyed much success, winning 246 games, while losing 82. His teams have been responsible for 9 Division titles, 3 League Championships, and 7 Section IV Crowns under his guidance. In 2001, UE captured its first-ever Class A State Title, and repeated that feat in 2003. "I have quite a big family", says Folls. "Not only am I blessed with my wonderful immediate family, but my players are my family too." That's a big family! What a large payoff for this "little guy" from UE.

Did You Know:
Folls is an avid reader of books about the Civil War, WWII and the Vietnam War.

14

Ed Folli

faces

Scott Gallagher

editor

Scott Gallagher is a native son of Johnson City. After obtaining an education at Broome Community College and SUNY Brockport, he returned home to take a job with WBNG-TV 12. He has worked for the station as a photographer, and he currently is the Assignment Editor. Scott has gained recognition for his innovation by winning the New York State Associated Press Award in 1995 for best news series, called "Consolidated Dollars and Sense." In 1998, the New York State Broadcasters Association honored him with First Place in the Best Enterprise News Story category.

The community has benefited greatly from Scott's concern for young people. He has served as Director of Recreation for the Village of Johnson City, providing youth programs for thousands of children. He was President of the J.C. Junior Basketball League. He founded the J.C. Boys and Girls Travel Basketball teams and coached the boys' team for several years. He also co-founded the J.C. Basketball Club, and founded the J.C. Pee Wee Football program.

Along with his abiding interest in youth sports programs, Scott has served on the Broome County Family Violence Prevention Council and the Medical Reserve Corps Ad Hoc Committee.

Wanting to make his hometown a safer place inspired Scott to graduate from the Johnson City Citizens Police Academy, and to serve as an elected leader on the J.C. School Board. In 2001, he was elected to the Johnson City Village Board as a Trustee and was a driving force in consolidating the 911 dispatch with Broome County. A great pride in the community he serves is reflected in all his endeavors. Scott and his family still reside in Johnson City, and he plans to continue serving the people of Broome County in diverse capacities.

"I'm hopeful that my many years of community service will have helped leave a mark here in our area", says Scott Gallagher.

Did You Know: Scott Gallagher is the founder of the JC boys and girls youth travel basketball teams, and the boys team won 36 straight games in 1997-98.

15

Scott Gallagher

faces

Don Giovanni

radio host

Don Giovanni is the warm, congenial voice folks have been hearing on the radio for the last twenty years. He has been a fan of the radio business since he was a small boy growing up in Chenango Bridge, and he credits his father with passing on the radio bug. His dad showed him the big radio towers on the mountaintops around Binghamton, and Don grew to love the towering beacons that blinked like red stars in the night.

Don traveled the country for a time in his youth, looking for fame and fortune, until he found his destiny back at home in Binghamton. With the encouragement of his wife, Colleen, he began to seriously pursue a career on the airwaves. For 14 years, he has created smiles and brought back memories by featuring the music of "Good Time Italian Oldies." This program promotes the preservation of Italian culture and has become a favorite with people of every age and heritage. Don Giovanni's voice is friendly and gentle, and encourages audience participation. Recently, Don has been installed as the morning DJ on the local station WINR-AM, hosting the *Crowley Morning Show – Celebrate Life with Don Giovanni*.

His connection with his audience goes beyond Greater Binghamton. With the creation of Don Giovanni's Italian Carousel, a syndicated radio program that has been delighting thousands all over the country for the past ten years, many people near and far can tune in and listen to Don's charm. His show is filled with nostalgic Italian music and the warm personality of its host.

Don has this to say about living and working in Binghamton: "It is such an honor to be invited into the homes, offices and cars in this wonderful valley. It is a privilege to entertain and inform so many people. That's the fun thing about radio for me. When I am in the studio, I can create a little theatre of the mind to share with each of you. And now, thanks to the nice photo taken by my good friend Ed Aswad, you get to see the real guy who comes into your lives each day...on the radio."

Did You Know:
Don was the last person to broadcast live from the famous Fountains Pavilion, in Johnson City.

16

Don Giovanni

Luigi Gobbo

tile maker

The life of Luigi Gobbo is a classic American immigrant success story. His early life in Italy was a continual financial struggle, so, in 1965, he came to the United States under the sponsorship of Attilio Trevisan, an employee of a local tile and marble company in Binghamton.

When Luigi arrived on American shores he had a small suitcase, thirty-five dollars, and abundant ambition and talent. Luigi learned English by taking classes at night school...and by enjoying Hollywood movies.

Luigi remained working and learning in the tile business until 1987, when he started his own tile contracting company. He became a master craftsman who takes pride in quality workmanship. His artistic talent was augmented by training in the mosaic arts at Motta di Livenza, in the province of Trevisio at La Scuola, Argentina.

His mosaic creations are displayed in many private and commercial collections. The Visions Credit Union in Watkins Glen, New York, commissioned two large wine country scenes for the outside of their building. St. John's Ukrainian Church in Johnson City owns a five-foot by eight-foot mosaic of a baptismal scene. Luigi worked for over a year on that magnificent work of art.

Luigi's wife and two children have provided the love and inspiration to continue his work in mosaics. His commitment to the local Sons of Italy organization has been consistent and he has served on their Board of Directors for several years.

In the near future, Luigi's eye for color and style will be put to good use when he opens his own mosaic studio on Oak Hill Avenue in Endicott. He will devote his full time and energy to creating large and small mosaics to enhance the aesthetics and imagination of our community.

Did You Know:
Luigi is a soccer fanatic, and his favorite team is AC Milan in Milan, Italy.

17

Luigi **Gobbo**

Bill Grace

rock-n-roll policeman

For 34 years, Bill Grace served with the Binghamton Police Department. What he is best known for is the 16 years he spent as the first Drug Abuse Resistance Education (D.A.R.E.) officer on the force. Using an energetic and unique blend of rock and roll, Officer Grace sang and danced and reached thousands of young people with his anti-drug, anti-alcohol and anti-violence message. D.A.R.E. became more than a job – it turned into a life mission to spread the values of peace, respect, and love through the safety of a drug-free existence.

Bill advocated physical, mental, and spiritual well-being through his own example of running, meditating, and practicing his faith. Schools, churches, and youth organizations took advantage of Grace's presentations to provide their youths with the guidance needed at impressionable ages.

Bill Grace inspired children to stand strong against negative influences by being a role model; offering care and friendship surrounded with music. Over the years, he has received recognition, awards and commendations for helping to protect our children and the future of our nation. The dozens of awards for his exemplary efforts include: WBNG-TV's Jefferson Award, the National Jefferson Award, the NY Lottery's New York State Educator of the Week, the NYS Moose Association's New York State Public Servant of the Year, the Binghamton Fire Department Community Service Award, and the NYS D.A.R.E. Officers Association's Officer of the Year Award.

After decades of faithfully serving the community on the Binghamton police force, Bill retired from the police department in 2004. He left a legacy that will last for generations, and Bill says he continues to thank God for giving him the opportunity to help the people of Binghamton. Today, he continues his efforts by working for Operation Weed and Seed, a U.S. Department of Justice community-based initiative. The program is an innovative and comprehensive multi-agency approach to law enforcement, crime prevention, and community revitalization.

Did You Know:
In 1966, Bill Grace set the record for the 100-yard dash and 1-mile run for Catholic Central High School.

18

Bill Grace

cartoonist

Johnny Hart is synonymous with his cartoon strip B.C. Filled with simple drawings and caveman gags - the strip was born in 1958. After initially being turned down by five syndicates before it was accepted for newspaper publication, it is now one of the best-known comics in the world. Images from B.C. are on products ranging from greeting cards to glassware. A collection of the comic strips has been published in five languages, and the strip has been adapted for television. Johnny's hilarious prehistoric characters have been chosen to represent many major companies in national advertising campaigns. He has even provided illustrations for the Olympic Games.

In his own words, Johnny describes himself as "wild and wacky," the very talents needed to augment his artistic gifts and turn him into one of the world's premier cartoonists. A lifelong resident of the Southern Tier, Johnny graduated from Union-Endicott High School. Soon afterward, he met Brant Parker, a cartoonist who became a prime influence in his life. Today, the two remain partners in the major syndicated comic strip The Wizard of Id.

The B.C. Open is an annual PGA golf tournament in Endicott named for Johnny's flagship creation. His B.C. characters wander through the tournament's advertising, program, sculptures on the course, and even on the winning trophy. For Johnny, the tournament is not just about golf; it is an extension of his belief in his hometown. "I do love this tournament and the magic of the community that makes it possible. I like to be part of the wonder that happens in Endicott at tournament time."

A great faith in the community led Johnny and his wife Bobby to coordinate with the Council of Churches and establish the Christian Prayer Breakfast during the B.C. Open. Johnny has been generous with permission to use his characters for many charitable events, and his drawings are a familiar sight throughout Broome County. A dashing dinosaur from B.C. welcomes visitors to many Broome County Parks. Johnny Hart's contributions to art and life will continue to bring Broome County and the world beyond closer together through the language of laughter.

Did You Know:
Johnny Hart named most of the characters in the B.C. comic strip after his friends.

19

Johnny Hart

Dr. Beverly Hosten

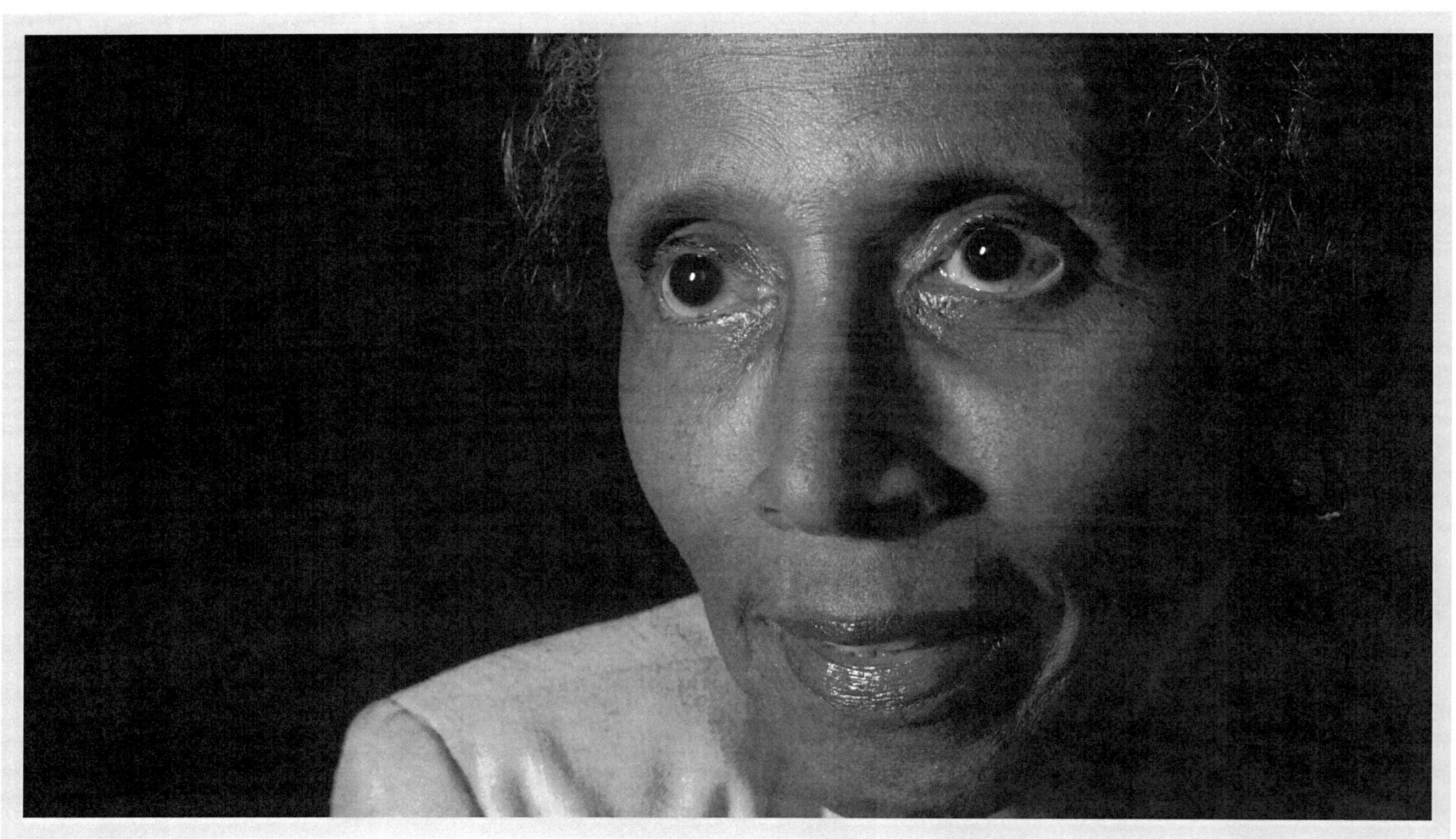

physician

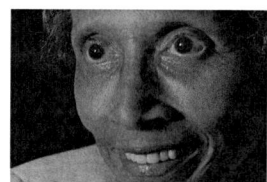

Dr. Beverly Hosten spent nearly thirty-seven years doing what she enjoyed best. She practiced internal medicine in Binghamton, helping countless patients through a private practice she shares with her husband, Dr. Beverly Dorsey. Dr. Hosten received her start with an internship and medical residency at Wilson Memorial Hospital in Johnson City. She then went on to Queens General Hospital in Jamaica, NY for her medical residency. Then Dr. Hosten returned to the Southern Tier, as part of the medical staff for Endicott Johnson Corporation, prior to teaming up with her husband.

Dr. Hosten was born and raised in New York City. She attended the Girl's High School in Brooklyn, NY, and graduated with honors. She pursued her higher education at Hunter College in New York City, before attending Howard University College of Medicine in Washington, D.C.

She has been extremely active, both within her field of medicine and in the larger community. Dr. Hosten has received numerous awards and honors, including the Chairman's Recognition Award in appreciation for service to the department of Internal Medicine at United Health Services Hospitals in 2000. She also received an Honorary Paul Harris Fellowship Distinguished Citizen Award from Rotary in 1999.

In addition, Dr. Hosten has served on numerous committees, such as the Board of Directors for United Health Services, the Council of Binghamton University as Advisor to the President, the United Fund for the United Way, and Physicians for Planned Parenthood. She also has served as the Medical Advisor for Broome County Home Health Care, and as a Trustee for the Children's Home of Wyoming Conference.

"My mother gave me the drive to be a professional person and my father taught me the importance of social consciousness and social justice", explained Dr. Hosten. And her parents taught her well. Her accomplishments are numerous, and her compassion for others is infinite.

Did You Know:
There are two Beverlys in the Dorsey home – both husband and wife have the same first name.

20

Beverly Hosten

Phil Jordan

psychic

In 1975 Police agencies throughout Tioga County were searching for a missing six-year old boy after he became lost in the dense woods during an August thunderstorm. According to a testimonial on philjordan.com, Phil Jordan led police to the boy within an hour of his involvement of the search. The testimonial goes on to explain that Phil used a map he envisioned the night before, and his mental capabilities to locate Tommy Kennedy after two hundred searchers were unsuccessful in their attempts. The boy was found completely safe and alive. Phil credits the find to his unique psychic abilities.

A short time after that day Phil was sworn in as a Deputy with the Tioga County Sheriff's Department where he is called on to assist in other cases. Phil's exceptional talent has earned him the respect of law enforcement departments throughout the country and the general public. He is well known for performing psychic readings for individuals and is constantly in demand. How does one know they have psychic abilities? Phil Jordan says he knew at an early age. "When I was sixteen years old I had a dream that my Uncle was going to have a heart attack. The very next day he did. From that day on I knew how my unconscious world would unfold. I was then able to perceive things about myself and other people".

However, Phil's interaction with the human spirit extends much further than his extrasensory talents. He is the holder of a Master of Science degree in Education from Elmira College. His thesis was written on the role of funeral services in the grief process. In 1988, he became licensed as a funeral director in New York State and currently owns the Candor Funeral Parlour, Inc. Phil continues his journey by offering service and comfort to those in need.

Phil is also a published author of a volume that offers his life experiences to those seeking to learn more about psychic abilities. The book is entitled *I Knew This Day Would Come: A Personal Journey to Psychic Self-Awareness*.

Did You Know:
Phil is an excellent dancer to 1940s and 1950s music.

21

Phil Jordan

artist/designer

Robert Keller is an original. In art and in his life his style is "romantic realism." He is a nationally recognized artist, designer, scholar and professor, and he is a prominent member of the cultural scene in New York State.

Born in Binghamton in 1925, he obtained a solid art and design education at the Pratt Institute in Brooklyn, the Art Students League in New York City, SUNY Cortland, and Binghamton University. His career in art was delayed by service in the Navy for two years during World War II, and then again by four years of service including the Korean War. After gaining experience in art and decorating in several locations around the United States, Robert Keller returned home to the Southern Tier. He became an elementary and secondary school art teacher. Next, he obtained a position as a professor at Broome Community College, where he taught for 30 years. He founded the Art and Design Department and was its director for 20 years. He earned emeritus status in 1991. Robert was also the first BCC Cultural Committee Chair and a Mentor at Empire State College.

Roberson Museum and Science Center in Binghamton enjoyed the privilege of his art instruction for 23 years. He was also curator of the Thornbrook Hall Museum for seven years. During this time he also maintained a busy volunteer life, in the Fine Arts Society, at the Binghamton Museum of Fine Arts, and as founder of the Rod Serling Memorial Foundation. One of his most memorable achievements was the innovation of the Binghamton Sidewalk of Stars. Robert has also sung in the Tri Cities Opera, was the first Docent Chair of the Phelps Mansion, and served on the boards of directors of numerous other cultural organizations.

Robert's most recent achievement was the publication of a book, *House Proud*, detailing adventures in his early life, as well as his experiences in restoring vintage houses in need of a loving touch. The themes of the book fit well with one of his primary goals: "As long as I live art and culture will be part of my being. And I hope some of this passion for preservation of our cultural heritage will have a lasting effect in Broome County."

Did You Know:
Robert has owned and restored six vintage homes.

22

Bob Keller

Guido LeBron

baritone

Baritone Guido LeBrón is a world renowned opera singer who has made his home in Binghamton since 1985. Born in San José, Costa Rica and raised in San Juan, Puerto Rico, he is the son of a trumpet player and a schoolteacher. Guido's childhood home was filled with all kinds of music that would influence the rest of his life. He became a professional Afro-Cuban jazz percussionist at the age of 15 and dreamt of making it his career.

After receiving a BA in Theatre Arts from Fordham University, and a MA in Theatre Technology from Binghamton University, his career took a different turn. David Clatworthy, professor of voice at BU, heard Guido sing and suggested that he become an opera singer rather than a theatre designer. In the years since he took that advice, Guido has been internationally acclaimed for his performances with leading opera companies in Spain, Ireland, Costa Rica, Puerto Rico, Mexico, Canada, Venezuela, and the United States in such roles as Scarpia in *Tosca*, Germont in *La Traviata*, Figaro in *The Barber of Seville* and the title role in *Rigoletto*. Recently, famed tenor Placido Domingo, Artistic Director of Washington National Opera at Kennedy Center, has taken a personal interest in Guido's career. This has lead to wide acclaimed performances as Scarpia and Riccardo in *I Puritani* with the company.

Locally, Guido has performed at the Anderson Center for the Arts, the Cider Mill Playhouse, Tri-Cities Opera and with the Binghamton Philharmonic. A well-known interpreter and proponent of zarzuela, the traditional Spanish art form, he is very active in the Binghamton community where he lives with his wife Julie and their daughter Sofía. He was recently named Artistic Director of Opera Cabaret of Endicott where he volunteers his time to share opera and Italian folk songs in an informal setting. In his time off Guido plays Afro-Cuban drums with local jazz groups and this brings him additional fulfillment in the world of music. Guido continues to enrich the Southern Tier with his exceptional talent and his admirable leadership. "This town and the people gave me so much when I was starting out. I travel all over and it's so nice to come back to a normal life here with such generous and genuine people. I owe this town, and I'll never forget the pay-back".

Did You Know: Guido's great uncle was Juan Tizol, the only Puerto Rican member of The Duke Ellington Band. He wrote the music for the song "Caravan".

23

Guido LeBron

Mark Levy

inventor

Interesting people do a multitude of interesting things, and in Mark Levy's case he does them all very well. He received his J.D. degree from New York Law School and is the principal attorney at the law firm of Mark Levy & Associates. The firm concentrates on intellectual and property law, a serious business according to Mark.

Mark says, "When you create an original work of art, such as a painting, photo, video, music, poem, lyrics, story, novel, screenplay, computer program or sculpture, the copyright law automatically protects it. That protection occurs immediately, upon creation. As a practical matter, though, you should place a copyright notice on the work and register it in the U.S. Copyright office. The main reason for doing this is that registration is a prerequisite to bringing a lawsuit for copyright infringement. Merely because it is ever easier to copy the works of others, via tape recorders, VCR's, photocopiers, and the Internet, for example, doesn't make it lawful to do so." Mark Levy has honed a compelling style of public speaking that has made him a sought-after lecturer in locations as far away as Missoula, Montana, and as close as Binghamton University. The topics include patents, trademarks, copyrights, and trade secrets. A Bachelor of Science degree in physics from Polytechnic University solidified Mark's lifelong interest in science. He has had articles published in the *Bulletin of Atomic Scientists, The New York Times, Videomaker Magazine, Symphony Magazine*, and the *American Orchid Society Bulletin*.

Mark's fascination with science led him to originate the "Invention Convention" for Binghamton Imaginink. It is now a statewide program that encourages students to create their own inventions. He continues to coordinate the local student invention program, and actively works to make the world a better place, beginning with Broome County. Mark maintains confidence in the Greater Binghamton area and its potential for growth, believing it is one of the best places to live and raise a family.

Did You Know:
Mark is an amateur movie maker and is currently the President of the Amateur MovieMakers Association.

24

Mark Levy

Senator Tom Libous

senator

A lifelong dedication to public service is the hallmark for Thomas W. Libous. Senator Libous is serving his ninth term in the New York State Senate representing Broome, Tioga and Chenango Counties.

A graduate of Broome Community College and the State University of New York at Utica, He worked in the private sector at Chase-Lincoln First Bank and the Johnson City Publishing Company. In 1988, his election to the NYS Senate set the course for his life as a political leader. But his course was hinted at years earlier, he explains. "I was only sixteen years old during the summer of 1969 when I phoned my uncle, Al Libous, for what would be my first political experience," the Senator said. "I told him that I wanted to help out on his mayoral campaign and would do anything I was asked. So he put me to work that summer and fall going door-to-door and learning about grassroots campaigning."

A little more than ten years later, Senator Libous became the Republican Party Chairman and County Vice-Chairman. He served as a City Councilman for the City of Binghamton before running for State Senate, where he has excelled. Senator Libous' compassion has extended to helping people with disabilities, particularly children. For several years he served as Chairman of the Mental Health and Developmental Disabilities Committee, and the Alcoholism and Drug Abuse Committee. Senator Libous also founded the *Senator Libous BOOKS Program* to encourage young people to read.

In 2005, Senate Majority Leader Joseph L. Bruno appointed Senator Libous to Chair the Transportation Committee, and to serve as Assistant Majority Leader for House Operations. To maintain and improve our quality of life, he has encouraged sports in the Southern Tier. He helped to convince the Ottawa Senators to locate its American Hockey League affiliate in Binghamton, maintained active support for the PGA's B.C. Open golf tournament in Endicott, and encouraged the AA level Binghamton Mets Baseball Club to continue to make the Southern Tier its home.

The region has greatly benefited from the service of Thomas Libous. He, his wife Frances, and their two grown sons have all participated in activities in the region he loves. As his tireless efforts continue, they will be remembered for years to come.

Did You Know:
Senator Libous' grandfather operated a store in Binghamton called the White House Candy Kitchen.

25

Tom **Libous**

Floyd Maines

entrepreneur

In 1919, a corporate dynasty was begun by selling penny candy. That was the year Floyd L. Maines, Sr. started a small business that employed just three people. The Maines Candy Company conducted sales from a small sample case, which was carried to local grocers. The average order was about twenty dollars.

Floyd L. Maines, Jr. graduated from Miami University in 1942, during the Second World War. He volunteered to serve five years in the United States Navy. His years in the Navy were spent with the Mine Disposal Branch, the Underwater Demolition Team, and the Navel Tech Intelligence Team. During his service years, Floyd also helped to organize the elite U.S. Navy Seals.

In 1947, a second generation joined the Maines family business. Although Floyd L. Maines, Jr. would have preferred to work with the FBI, his father talked him into selling candy. Floyd Jr. expanded the business in new directions to capitalize on the popularity of corner drug stores and soda fountains. The name of the corporation soon changed to Maines Candy and Paper Company.

Today, the business has grown into a billion dollar corporation run by a third Maines generation – Floyd's sons David and Bill. Due to unprecedented growth, a second distribution center was opened in Cleveland, Ohio in 1987. This facility serviced the mid-west region of multi-unit accounts. Then, By 1999, a 360,000 square foot, world-class distribution center was constructed and became the Corporate Headquarters for Maines Paper & Food Service, Inc. This state-of-the-art facility has five temperature zones and temperature controlled shipping/receiving docks. It is equipped with a fully functional Test Kitchen and Learning Center for product cuttings, menu roll-outs and training sessions. The company is a major employer in Broome County, providing jobs for 700 people. Floyd maintains that he is semi-retired, but he is still active in running Maines Paper & Food Service, Inc., while enjoying part of the year in Florida.

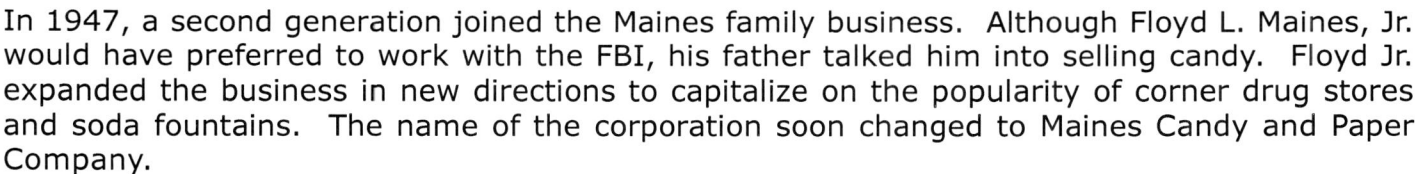

Did You Know:
Floyd was a frog-man during WWII.

26

Floyd Maines

Tony Mitchell

Tony Mitchell

dancer

Anthony Stephen Mitchell has packed a lot of experiences into his sixteen years. He currently holds the title of Mr. Acrobat of Central New York, and the national title of Mr. Acrobat of the United States. At the age of nine, Tony began studying at the Lighthouse Academy of Dance, excelling in Acro-dance. In 2003, Tony was accepted into the touring group "The Young Continentals" and spent six weeks singing and dancing in Christian-oriented performances. The group traveled from Kansas City to Montreal, entertaining at a different church or school every evening.

Tony is now a theatre veteran who made his stage debut at the age of five. He was an original cast member of the television shows *Down on Noah's Ark* and *Sunday School Rock*, local cable access television shows. When Tony was six years old he auditioned for *Babes in Toyland.* The audition song he selected was the US ARMY theme song "Be All That You Can Be". This caught the director off guard and Tony was selected to participate in the show.

In addition to being an honor student in his junior year at Chenango Valley High School, he is active in various organizations and clubs, including the Alcohol and Drug Student Information Program. He also volunteers with a student-run coffee house.

Tony is active in his church youth group and community service projects such as the riverbank cleanup. He has also participated in an evangelistic retreat called Students Equipped to Minister to their Peers. Plans for Tony's future include studying architecture in college and continuing to study, and eventually teach and of course – dance.

Did You Know:
Tony has been a Boy Scout since the third grade and is currently working on becoming an Eagle Scout.

27

Tony **Mitchell**

sports announcer

Roger Neel is a trusted voice in the world of Binghamton radio. With his rich, deep, carefully modulated voice, Roger conveys a sense of strength and honesty. Currently he is the Program and Sports Director for WNBF-AM and WYOS-AM (Citadel Broadcasting), and the morning show host for WNBF Newsradio.

Growing up on a poultry farm in Western Pennsylvania ingrained a strong work ethic in Roger. He credits his parents as positive influences during those early years. His father always told him, "If you want to eat – you work." His father also encouraged Roger to pursue his interests in athletics and broadcasting.

Roger graduated from Westminster College in New Wilmington, Pennsylvania, with a B.A. in Speech and Broadcasting. Roger also played baseball and football, earning honors and gaining the respect of Dr. Harold Burry, Westminster's head football coach. Roger credits Dr. Burry with inspiring him to "meet a higher level, everyday, in everything I do."

Roger has been the voice of many local sports teams, including his play-by-play commentary for the Broome Dusters in the American Hockey League where he got his start. When the Dusters became the Binghamton Whalers he continued to call those games for six years. He was given the James H. Ellery Award for outstanding radio coverage of the American Hockey League for 1985, and was admitted to the Binghamton Hockey Hall of Fame in 2003. He has been the voice of Binghamton University's men's basketball team for the past eight seasons.

Roger's deep commitment to family and community is obvious. He donates time to the American Heart Association and CHOW, and is president of the Broome Sports Foundation.

Roger considers himself fortunate to have met so many wonderful people through broadcasting and athletics.

Did You Know:
Roger played college baseball with teammate Darryl Jones, who went on to play for the New York Yankees.

28

Roger Neel

producer

For more than thirty years, Albert Nocciolino's life has been a celebration of the theatrical arts. He is President and CEO of NAC Enterprises, Ltd., a company he founded in 1976. NAC Enterprises is a diversified entertainment and theatrical company specializing in the presentation of national touring Broadway shows in New York State and Pennsylvania.

Much of Albert's business is conducted in other cities, from Buffalo to New York City, and many locations between. However, he and his family have chosen to live in Binghamton. Albert says he is fortunate to be able to maintain a home in a small community and still be within easy travel distance to major entertainment centers. As he puts it, "This is a wonderful place to raise a family and I like being here. The quality of life is spectacular."

Some of Albert's recent Broadway and off Broadway producing credits include the 2002 Six Time Tony winning *Thoroughly Modern Millie* along with *Rent* and *De La Guarda*. Current touring productions include *The Full Monty* and *Thoroughly Modern Millie.* Some of his past producing credits include *Guys and Dolls starring Maurice Hines, Annie, Peter Pan starring Cathy Rigby, West Side Story, Jelly's Last Jam, The Great Radio City Spectacular starring the Rockettes, FAME, A Chorus Line: The Broadway Tour of America, Dreamgirls, Six Degrees of Separation*, the Pulitzer-Prize winning play *The Piano Lesson*, and *The Fantasticks* starring Robert Goulet.

Over the years, Albert has received two Tony Awards, a star on the Binghamton Sidewalk of Fame, and the Lifetime Achievement Award from the Broome County Arts Council. He has been a member of the Committee of the League of American Theatres & Producers, and a founding member and Chairman of the National Touring Theatre Council. Serving on the Binghamton University Council Board has been a particularly rewarding experience for him, as was serving on numerous other local boards of directors.

All of his success hasn't dampened his enthusiasm for our area. Here's how he describes it: "I love Italian food and I love to collect good wine, and there is nowhere better to get both than right here in Broome County."

Did You Know:
Albert likes to collect Italian cookbooks.

29

Albert **Nocciolino**

coach

Binghamton University's campus abounds with exceptional staff. Even among the best, Jim Norris is a stand out. He is in his 15th year at BU, and his sixth year as Associate Athletic Director of Non-Revenue Programs. He provides direct oversight to BU's 19 Non-Revenue teams, the Sports Medicine Division, the Strength and Conditioning Program, and the Support Systems Operation (SSO).

Notable accomplishments during his tenure include the addition of the men's and women's lacrosse programs and the complete restructuring of the Sports Medicine and SSO Divisions. The Non-Revenue programs have contributed significantly toward winning the America East Conference Academic Cup in two of the last four years.

Jim came to Binghamton University in 1991, becoming the top assistant coach to Dick Baldwin for five years. In all, he has coached basketball for 26 years. Prior to taking over at BU in 1996, he spent seventeen years as a park and recreation administrator at the City of Binghamton and later at Broome County.

"The change from coaching to administration has allowed me to make a greater impact on a larger number of student-athletes here at B.U. We now have over 400 kids participating in these non-revenue programs and that's rewarding for me", says Jim Norris. With the intensity and integrity that have defined this life-long resident of Binghamton, Jim helped build a top-notch Division III program at BU in the early 1990s. Then he took over the Head Coach position during the University's historic transition to NCAA Division I.

Jim is also active in the community. He donates time for speaking engagements, serves on several boards of directors, and is actively involved with the youth programs at St. Paul's Church, where he coaches youth basketball. In 2001, he was honored with Binghamton-Vestal Sertoma's prestigious Man of the Year Award.

Did You Know:
Jim loves to sing his own version of the Notre Dame Fight song.

30

Jim Norris

martial arts master

Hidy Ochiai, a native of Japan and a U.S. citizen, came to the United States in 1962 with the mission of teaching the martial arts. In 1966, after receiving his B.A. from Albright College, Master Ochiai moved to Binghamton, NY and established Washin-ryu (*wa*–harmony, *shin*–truth) Karate-do in the United States. Washin-ryu now includes 27 branch schools across the United States.

Considered to be a living legend in the martial arts, he has been inducted into the Black Belt Hall of Fame, as "Man of the Year," and as "Instructor of the Year," as well as to the Martial Arts History Museum Hall of Fame in Los Angeles. A pioneer in the field of character education and a true humanitarian, Hidy Ochiai has founded two non-profit organizations; Hidy Ochiai Foundation and the Educational Karate Program, which has been validated by the NYS Education Department. These organizations promote the principals of non-violence and self-development, while teaching safety awareness, self-respect and self-discipline.

Hidy Ochiai is the author of five books, including two comprehensive texts on self-defense. His most recent book, *A Way to Victory: Miyamoto Musashi's Book of Five Rings* is an English translation and commentary of Musashi's ancient text and represents a seven-year effort to render the wisdom and spirit of Musashi's timeless teachings. Hidy Ochiai believes, "My true role is that of a 'teacher'. My subject is human development, as it allows people to live together harmoniously."

Master Ochiai chooses to direct his activities from his home in Broome County. "Within twelve months of opening in 1966, I had more than one-hundred students. When I mentioned I might move [to LosAngeles or New York City] many of my students said they would follow. Not wanting to disrupt their lives I decided to stay in the Southern Tier. It's not where you live, it's how you live." For over forty years, Master Ochiai has helped individuals reach their potential in life and to live in harmony with others.

The foundation of Hidy Ochiai's teaching is... "The human spirit is a spiral which can go up or down by the application of our free will... but it can not remain stagnant. The Martial Arts are a beautiful tool for teaching the human spirit how to spiral upward. What else really matters, other than helping each other to realize our human potential as we spiral upward just as a *Dragon in Clouds*."

Did You Know:
Hidy Ochiai took up the sport of golf for the first time at the age of 55.

31

Hidy Ochiai

Barbara Oldwine

model citizen

Barbara Harris Oldwine was the first African-American caseworker for the city of Binghamton in 1947. From there, she progressed to Supervisor of the Medicaid Unit at the Broome County Social Services Department. Barbara was also a teacher of Field Human Resources at Broome Community College, and she hosted a talk show on WICZ television.

Barbara was born and raised in Binghamton, a time when the civil rights movement was at its peak. Barbara says, "They burned a cross on the hill on South Mountain the year I was born. My father never let me forget it; he always said to 'pay attention.' My parents were interested in civil rights and they would attend meetings at the community-founded Interracial Association at the YWCA. Later, the Association bought the building at 45 Carroll St. and it became the Urban League. My parents and the parents of my childhood close friend, Melba Lewis, were very active and also were involved in the founding of the local chapter of the NAACP".

Upon her graduation from North H.S. in 1941, Barbara attended Fisk University in Nashville, TN where she earned a Bachelor of Arts degree as a history major in 1945. She married Cornelius Vernon Oldwine Jr., on D-Day, June 6, 1944. As her professional career began Barbara took her work and community service very seriously and never looked back. Her strength of purpose and charisma were widely recognized when Barbara worked through dozens of organizations and boards to champion various causes. In recognition of her accomplishments, Binghamton's Mayor Richard Bucci appointed her to the Community Development Committee.

She has also received many awards, including: the National Association of Social Workers' Public Citizen Award (New York Chapter, Southern Tier Division), the State University of New York Board of Trustees' Distinguished Citizen Award, New York Governor Mario Cuomo's African-American of Distinction Award, the NYS Broadcaster of the Year Award, Binghamton's Bicentennial Woman of the Year Award, and the Broome County Bar Association's Liberty Bell Award.

Barbara is dedicated to freedom, democracy and diversity. As the granddaughter of freed slaves, she has used her heritage to be a beacon to those in need. She has acted as an advocate for people of all cultural and socio-economic backgrounds.

Did You Know:
Barbara is a world traveler, visiting Africa, Russia, England, Philippines, Hong Kong and Jordan.

32

Barbara Oldwine

Marla Olmstead

artist - 5 years old

Like very few people in this world, the artist Marla is recognized by her first name alone. The fact that Marla is only five years old makes this especially amazing. Marla's sophisticated abstract paintings have captured the attention of collectors and the media worldwide. Her paintings sell for thousands of dollars apiece.

Marla began painting before her second birthday. She was given a brush to keep her entertained so her father could paint as a hobby. Very quickly "it became more her passion than my passion," explains her father, Mark Olmstead. She soon became a prolific artist and the canvasses got larger.

In June 2004, local businessman Wayne Kerber was fasinated by Marla's work and bought a piece for a couple of hundred dollars. He brought the painting to the attention of professional artist and gallery owner Anthony Brunelli (see pg. 12). Brunelli was immediately captivated, and arranged the first major showing of her work at his Anthony Brunelli Fine Arts Gallery. The exhibit broke attendance records at the gallery.

The rest is history. At the age of four, Marla reached households around the world as she appeared in numerous newspapers, magazines and television programs. She is so well-known and sought after that a Google search for the name "Marla" brings up young Marla Olmstead as the top result. She has her own website where her works can be viewed at www.marlaolmstead.com.

The colors used in Marla's art are brilliant, and the style is uninhibited - just the way a five year-old's art should be. But her paintings have a tremendous amount of depth, nuance, and layering. The demand for her paintings is great, but she paints at her own pace – when and if she feels like having fun with the bright acrylic colors.

Today, Marla's paintings are owned by people all over the United States, and the world is quietly waiting to see what Marla will create as she grows older. In the meantime, she is a happy five year-old girl attending school and enjoying life with her parents and younger brother in Broome County.

Did You Know:
Marla loves to cook and watches The Food Network daily.

33

Marla

James Orband

attorney

James W. Orband is a native of the Southern Tier, and is currently the Managing Partner of Hinman, Howard & Kattell, LLP. Life in his home community helped him develop determination and resolve, along with a strong work ethic. These values were honed during his education at Binghamton University, where he graduated Magna Cum Laude. A J.D. degree Cum Laude from the Albany Law School of Union University completed his formal education. James is licensed to practice law in the States of New York, Pennsylvania and Florida, as well as the District of Columbia and the United States Tax Court. His legal practice focuses on banking, construction, corporate law, and mergers and acquisitions.

After practicing law in Florida, James returned to Binghamton in 1986. He and his wife are raising three children here because, as he explains, "This is a good place to live. I have many friends and clients whom I have known most of my life. There is always something to do in Greater Binghamton – from sports, to the arts, to great festivals." Believing that his good fortune should be reinvested in the community, he serves in many organizations, such as Catholic Charities of Broome County, and the Lourdes Hospital Foundation. He is also a Director of the Greater Binghamton Coalition, and was the Chairman of the Local Organizing Committee for the 2004 Empire State Games. He is associated with numerous professional groups, and volunteers as a director for several charitable foundations.

James acted on his firm faith in the future of this area when he became a principle in the organization of Endicott Interconnect Technologies. He expresses his optimism this way: "We have a great deal of pride in this community and we could not let the opportunity pass to retain a great number of jobs and invest in an exciting business opportunity. Revitalization is imminent. There will be significant development within the next five years in the Triple Cities. I can assist in preserving a positive way of life in Broome County, and it's the right thing to do. This area has been good to me, so it is time to make sure there will be good prospects for tomorrow's residents."

Did You Know:
Jim is a huge Perry Mason fan, with a collection containing every available episode on DVD.

34

James Orband

faces

35 | Dave Pessagno

events coordinator

"Life is not measured by the breaths you take, but how many times it takes your breath away." That is Dave Pessagno's favorite saying, and it is very fitting if you know his psyche. An extension of his favorite saying that he left out is that he also likes to take the breath away of those who attend his events. He's involved with so many large events in the area that it's a wonder he even has time to take a breath in between.

Dave is a professional events coordinator, and he is in very high demand. The reason for that demand is that every event he oversees enjoys tremendous success. He choreographs July Fest in downtown Binghamton, the Spiedie Fest Balloon Rally at Otsiningo Park, the Press Room at the B.C. Open, and the DBI Tennis Challenger Tournament at Binghamton's Recreation Park. He also coordinates countless events for organizations such as the Greater Binghamton Chamber of Commerce and Catholic Charities of Broome County. He also helps to serve over 5,000 needy people at the Holiday Thanksgiving Drive and organizes a drive to provide 2,500 needy children with toys and clothing.

Sports were always a big part of David's life, and his dedication paid off early, when he received a football scholarship for his athletic abilities out of Binghamton Central High School in 1977. He graduated from Drake University in Des Moines, Iowa in 1981. As a student there, he received the Drake D. Award, given to an outstanding athlete for their contributions to the Athletic Department as well as the larger community.

When asked how he shuffles so many large events over the course of the year, Dave responds modestly by saying, "I surround myself with good people. From the volunteers to the Board of Directors (of the various agencies), I perform my best when in good company."

Did You Know:
Growing up, Dave always dreamed of becoming a Hollywood stunt man.

35

Dave **Pessagno**

faces

Nancy Phillips

marketing executive

The Greater Binghamton area has benefited greatly from the work of Nancy H. Phillips. She has been the Corporate Director of Marketing for Vornado Realty Trust since 2003. She is responsible for marketing the Vornado portfolio of shopping malls, with properties in New York, New Jersey, Virginia, and Puerto Rico. Her position also includes Marketing Manager and Assistant Mall Manager at the Oakdale Mall in Johnson City.

Under Nancy's leadership, the Oakdale Mall has gone through a complete renovation bringing it up to date since it resurrected in 1975. The mall attracts an average of 80,000 visitors each week and is home to more than 100 retail businesses. Nancy continues to attract new stores to the mall adding to the growing list of improvements under her direction.

However, this is only one part of Nancy's persona. Her commitment and service to the Southern Tier have been formidable. There are many not-for-profit organizations that owe their very existence to her dedicated service. The complex duties of managing and marketing shopping malls in several locations has not kept Nancy from serving on boards of directors for the Binghamton University Foundation, the Broome Community College Foundation, the Harpur Forum, the Binghamton Symphony, Broome County Community Charities, First Night International, and the Discovery Center of the Southern Tier.

Being a multi-talented woman, Nancy has also self-published a book of quotes, entitled *Mallwalker Wisdom*. Her honors include the Binghamton University Foundation's Volunteer of the Year Award, the Broome County Arts Council's Patron of the Arts Award, the Jefferson Award, and numerous other symbols of recognition from a grateful community. The most important of these may be the naming of "The Phillips Gallery" at the Discovery Center for her many contributions.

Did You Know:
Nancy is a patron of the arts for up and coming young artists.

36

Nancy **Phillips**

Kathi Roberts

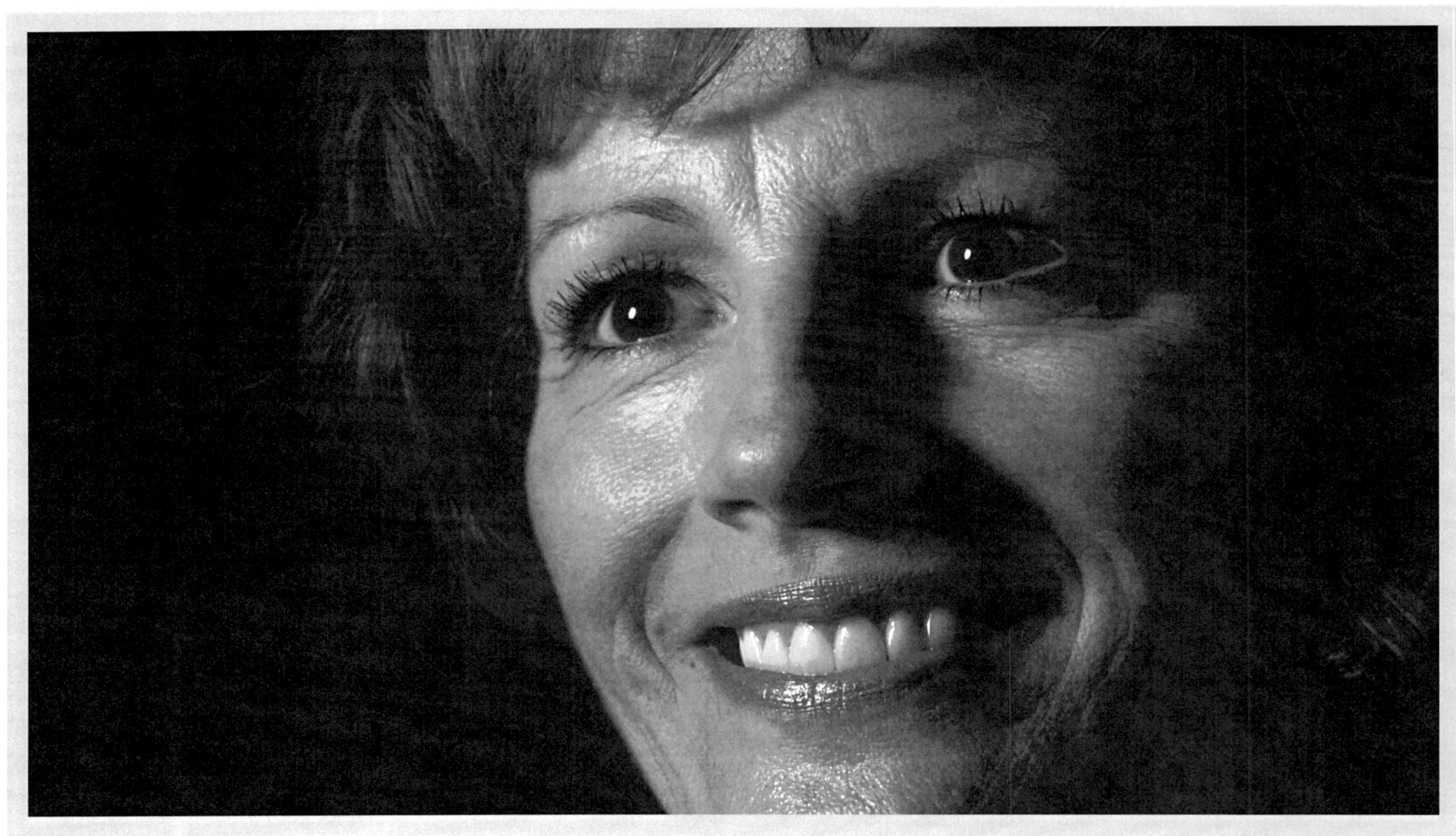

practice administrator

Kathi Roberts began working in the Southern Tier at Singer Link upon her graduation from college, and continued her computer science work on the space shuttle simulator in Singer Link's Houston, Texas facility. After returning to the area, she was employed by IBM for another 17½ years.

In 1994, Kathi joined her husband Dr. George Roberts at Roberts Eyecare Associates, as Practice Administrator. Their business became the focus of her professional life. It was named one of twelve best practices in the United States and received the Safilo Platinum Award. She and Dr. Roberts were awarded the Greater Binghamton Chamber of Commerce Small Business Persons of the Year in 2005. *The Binghamton Press & Sun-Bulletin* has also voted them "Best in Vision Care" several years in a row.

Kathi has also served the community through her involvement in the Vestal Rotary, the United Way, Relay for Life, the Community Foundation Board, and the Harpur Forum. Her graduation from the Broome Leadership Institute advanced Kathi's commitment to business and community, and she continues to participate in local charitable endeavors and health fairs. Kathi's goal of obtaining the latest in computerized instrumentation to support their business blends well with her personal philosophy of "supporting the community we live in, and being committed to staying in this area."

Kathi explains Roberts Eyecare will continue to invest in the community when they open their new office in Vestal. Being located on the Vestal Parkway is something she's always wanted to do. "We're excited to open our new facility with improved visiblity in the community", states Kathi. After all, improving visibilty is what their practice does best.

Did You Know:
Kathi attends every BU Bearcats game and just may be their biggest fan.

37

Kathi Roberts

Dr. I.J. Rosefsky

physician

Dr. Israel J. Rosefsky was born in 1910, and continues to fill every day of his life with humor, emotion, and an abiding quest for knowledge. From his childhood, he planned to become a doctor. Adversities were many for the aspiring physician, but through working hard from the time he was 6 years old, he met his goal and became a physician. Over the years, he added philanthropist, artist, world traveler and loving husband and father to his list of successful roles.

For 58 years, Dr. Rosefsky served the families of Broome County as a pediatrician, treating each child and parent with equal measures of expertise and compassion. Over the years, more than 13,500 newborn babies came under his care, and many remained under his care until they turned sixteen. His progressive, holistic philosophy of caring for the whole child, and monitoring development of the child at every stage of growth, engendered the confidence of parents. This rapport with both infant and parent generated a loyalty that lasted generations. "In my day we were able to spend more time with our patients and I was able to get to know the families fairly well. Today, of course, it's different times... I miss those days", says Dr. Rosefsky.

At the age of 50, Dr. Rosefsky's wife Elsie convinced him to paint. He began creating impressive, modernist, abstract works of art. His interest in painting continues into his current 95th year, and has led to numerous prestigious exhibitions. The death of his beloved wife in 1986 inspired Dr. Rosefsky to found the Elsie Benensohn Rosefsky Gallery at Binghamton University.

Scholarships, temple donations, a newborn nursery at Lourdes hospital, the Day Care Center at the Jewish Community Center, and an education room at the Roberson Museum & Science Center are just a few of his benevolent gifts to the community. His years are many and his memories are long, but Dr. I. J. Rosefsky is a man of today who is still looking forward to tomorrow.

Did You Know:
Dr. Rosefsky started a Men's Breakfast Club that met every week for 20 years.

38

Dr. Rosefsky

David Rossie

writer/author

People look forward to reading David Rossie's column in *The Binghamton Press & Sun-Bulletin* - either to praise him or to rant about him. Either way, Dave's comments inspire thought. Here's how he describes his column: "When writing, I never pick on the defenseless. I was told once that it was the job of the press to comfort the afflicted and afflict the comfortable." And that he does. When reading a Rossie column, the old song by Frank Sinatra comes to mind – "I Did It My Way."

While getting his education at Cortland State University, Dave planned to become a teacher. But by his junior year, he knew his future was in writing. In 1955, he began newspaper work at the *Binghamton Sun*, earning the grand salary of $55 a week. Today, he is the Associate Editor of the *Press & Sun-Bulletin*, and thanks to his regular column, he is one of the most well-known names in the Southern Tier.

Dave has been recognized for his writing with two H. L. Mencken Awards, and he was a Pulitzer Prize finalist in 1983. A writer of his caliber could have lived anywhere in the country. But, as he puts it, "I like this community, it's full of optimists. It has been a good place to raise my family."

Reflecting on his life, and that of his community, Dave says, "If had my life to re-live, I might want to be more involved in public service – or write more humor. People need to laugh. I do worry about the future. I think people are becoming non-readers. I believe there is danger in the loss of small farms, and I hate to see the downtown districts shrivel up. As far as the world situation goes, it is time to win friends for the United States again."

David Rossie's purpose in life may be deeper than he realizes, as he stimulates conversation and battles apathy. Another Sinatra song comes to mind: "For what is a man, what has he got, if not himself then he is not." David Rossie writes what he believes…and does it his way.

Did You Know:
David is the consummate outdoorsman, but is no novice around the kitchen. David Rossie loves to bake.

39

David Rossie

devoted volunteer

In 2004, Lana K. Rouff was designated a Woman of Distinction by the Indian Hills Girl Scouts. She has been involved with the Girl Scouts, Indian Hills Chapter, all her life and served as the chairperson for the 75th Anniversary. Her life and career have manifested a deep concern for the welfare of others.

Lana received her bachelor's degree from Case-Western Reserve University in Cleveland, Ohio. She went on to earn her Master of Arts degree in Theatre from Binghamton University.

Lana is well known for her warmth and for the efficiency she brings to every project she tackles, both as a professional and as a volunteer. At the Binghamton Philharmonic, she has served as Educational Coordinator, Development Coordinator, and Executive Director, lending new dimensions of competence to this popular musical company.

She has also served as a board member and president of the Binghamton University Foundation, and has been a member of the Binghamton University Athletic Council, and the Binghamton Rotary Club. As chairperson of the All Wars Memorial Committee, she has demonstrated a passion for honoring those who served the United States during times of war.

Lana has been recognized as a woman of achievement whose leadership inspires others to serve the community. Her commitment has been honored with the presentation of the Harpur College Alumni Award and the Jefferson Award.

Family is an important factor in Lana's life, and she and her husband raised their children in a community that has been enriched by their presence.

Did You Know:
Since childhood, Lana has been taking classical ballet lessons 2-3 times per week.

40

Lana **Rouff**

Michael "Jingles" Rubino

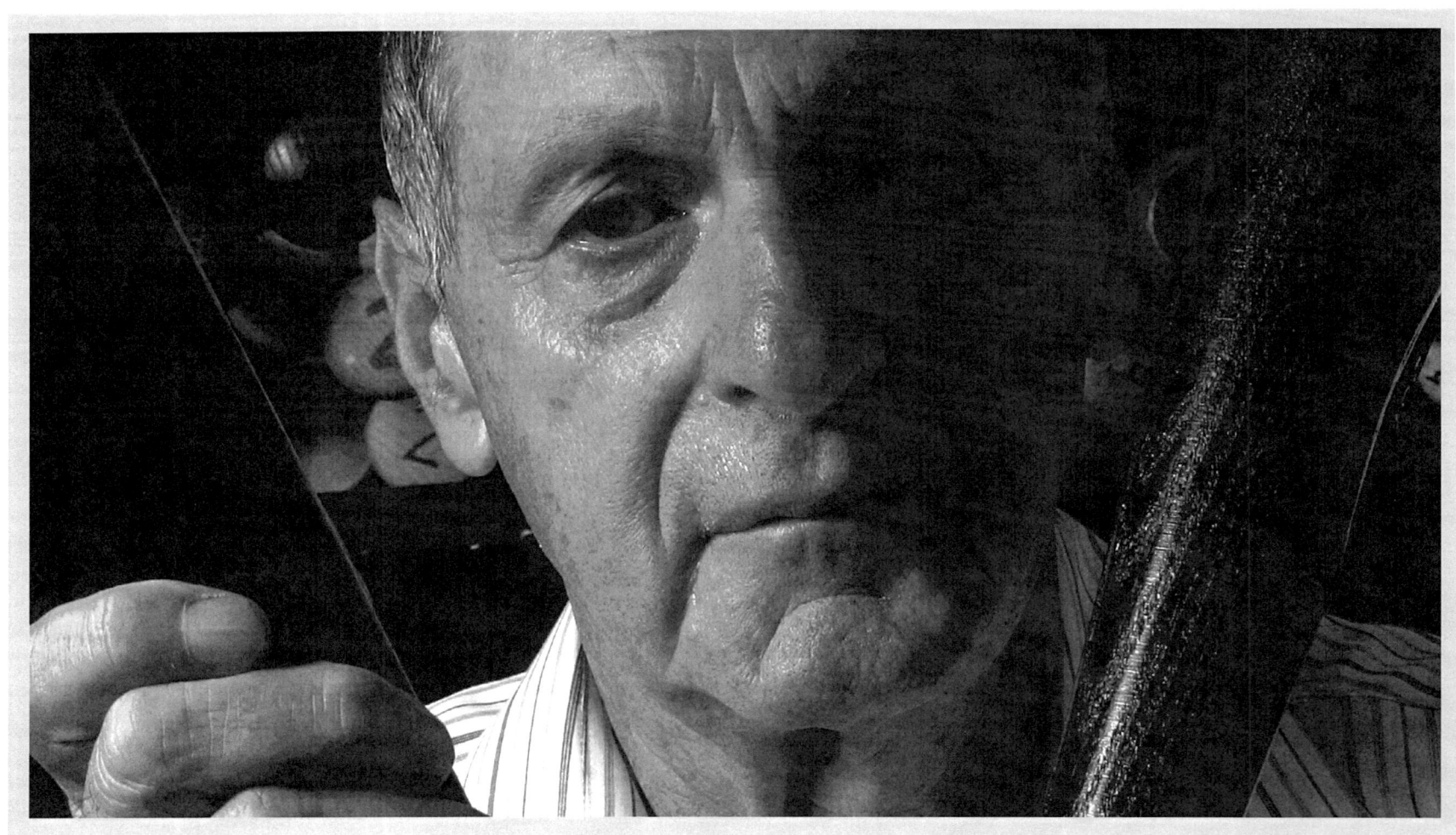

sports fan

There are ultimate sports fans in every city across the country, but chances are there's only one named "Jingles." Michael Rubino has been a staple at virtually every baseball park, ice rink, basketball court and football field around the Southern Tier for over forty years. You can see him dancing at NYSEG Stadium, shouting at the opposition at the Arena (at a Binghamton Senators games) or causing some commotion with the officials, coaches, and at times, players at a game. But deep down, Jingles has a true passion and great respect for sports.

Growing up in Dunmore, Pennsylvania, Jingles liked to play a game called sponge-ball. Sponge-ball is a version of baseball that is played without gloves and bats. "You have to remember, I'm getting up there in age," Jingles explains. "When I was a kid, we didn't have bats and gloves, so we played with a hard sponge-ball and hit the ball with our fists and caught with our bare hands. Every day before I left to play, I would take two pennies with me to go to the candy store. One penny was for a Mary Jane and the other was for a bubble gum. When I ran the bases, the other kids would hear the pennies jingle in my pocket and from there started calling me Jingles. The name stuck with me ever since."

Not only did the name stick, but it turned out to be the perfect name for the ultimate sports fan who can't sit still or keep quiet during a game. Jingles says he loves the excitement of a game and gets deeply involved in it. He wants the home team to have every advantage it can and will shout almost anything (without crossing the line) to try and psych out the opposition.

Jingles is also an umpire for baseball and softball, and has been since the 1960s. He has umpired thousands of Little League, Babe Ruth, and high school games, as well as countless men's softball games. He says he will continue to umpire as long as his health permits.

Jingles played high school baseball and basketball at Dunmore High School in Pennsylvania. He served in the U.S. Navy for four years, and then went on to work for Singer Link before putting in thirty-eight years at Anitec (formerly Ansco and GAF). He says he was brought up very strictly in the Catholic Church and continues to practice his faith to this day. He attends mass at St. Mary's of the Assumption parish in Binghamton. When asked what he likes to do for fun, Jingles says, "I like to pick and go to the best high school game of the week." We're not surprised. And don't expect to see Jingles at the BINGO hall too soon – unless he's the one calling out the numbers.

Did You Know:
Jingles served in the Korean War and was stationed on the Alan D. Sumner Destroyer.

41

Jingles

Bernie Shifrin

music instructor

Bernard J. Shifrin has been involved in teaching, conducting, and performing music in the Southern Tier for more than five decades. After attaining a B.S and M.S. in Music from Ithaca College, he began teaching music to students in the Binghamton School District in 1945.

Since that time, Bernard has had a profound influence on hundreds, and perhaps thousands, of young people interested in exploring the joy of music. He was influential in establishing the Binghamton Youth Symphony, and conducted this prestigious organization for 34 years. The group is a select assemblage of students from approximately 20 school districts. Competition for slots in the Youth Symphony is fierce, and the chance to perform with the group has always been considered a great honor.

Whenever a new school year began, Bernard advised his students to maintain an active love and interest in music as an avocation, and not as a profession. Fortunately, many of his students ignored the warning and became music teachers and performers themselves. Bernard has three daughters who also have become accomplished musicians. Bernard performed with and conducted the Binghamton Philharmonic Band, a professional organization, for more than 40 years. He also found time to form and conduct the Temple Israel Choir, retaining the conductor position for 40 years. He has also donated countless hours as a trustee of Temple Israel, as an active member of the Binghamton Kiwanis Club, and as a board member of many musical organizations.

In honor of his many years of cultural contributions, Bernard was awarded a star on the Binghamton Sidewalk of Fame. He credits his caring wife and children for making his music and leisure accomplishments possible. He also says that tennis, golf, and being an honorary member of the Binghamton Garden Club have honed his appreciation of strength and beauty.

Bernard sums up his life this way: "I have been blessed in so many facets of life, and I hope I have passed on some of this blessing to others."

Did You Know:
Bernie is a propagator of Dahlia and Canna plants. He gave away over 500 plants this year.

42

Bernie Shifrin

Gerald Smith

historian

Gerald Smith has built his career on the study and promotion of history. Born in Broome County, he received an A.A. degree in Liberal Arts from Broome Community College, and B.A and M.A. degrees in history from Binghamton University. He has served as the City of Binghamton's Official Historian since 1984, and as Broome County Historian since 1988.

Gerald's writing talent has been put to use in the production of several volumes, including *Valley of Opportunity: A Pictorial History of the Greater Binghamton Area*. He served as the editor of *Ogden's Observations: Sketches of Life in Binghamton and Broome County*, by William H. Ogden. He has written more than 200 articles for local newspapers. His love of local history was obvious as he narrated and hosted *At the Confluence: A Video Postcard of Binghamton and Broome County*.

Gerald was a major proponent of the establishment of a Broome County Local History & Genealogy Center in the Broome County Public Library, and he has been the head of the facility since 2000. He was responsible for the consolidation of historic records for Binghamton and Broome County into this central repository, which serves more than 40,000 researchers each year. He has served as a board member and president of the Association of Public Historians of NYS. Many other history societies have also benefited from his participation. The New York State Museum presented Gerald with the Edmund J. Winslow Local Government Historian's Award for Excellence.

A reputation as an entertaining and informative speaker has put Gerald in high demand. He presents more than 50 programs each year, and contributes to news broadcasts and local documentaries. He was also the head researcher and writer for the Visitor Centers in Binghamton and Endicott.

When asked why he has made this area his lifelong home, Gerald says, "This community is the right size for my family. We have all the benefits of city and rural life. We can live in relative safety and indulge in interests such as art and antiques. As for the future, the area has shown slow but consistent growth. With dynamic and positive government leadership, the area can once again be the 'Parlor City.' There is such a rich and diverse past in the Southern Tier – it will certainly be repeated in the years to come."

Did You Know:
Gerald is a miniature golf enthusiast, and has played at well over 100 courses.

43

Gerald Smith

Ray Stanton, II

quarterback/businessman

Raymond Henry Stanton, II likes to do things in twos. After all, it's part of his name. During the years 1970 – 1978, Ray founded, coached and played quarterback for the popular and entertaining TC Jets football team. In 1997 and 1998, he formed the B.C. Jets and did it all over again. His passion for football, his family, and his business seem to rub off on those around him in a profound way.

Ray came from humble beginnings. He was born on the East Side of Binghamton, and has spent most of his life there. From his early years, Ray was always a leader. He was president of his North High School class in 1961, and was the starting quarterback for their football team that same year. He went to prep school to play football for the Augusta Military Academy in Virginia. After returning to New York, he graduated from Cortland State in 1967, with a Bachelor of Science degree in Mathematics. In 1981, he received his Master of Arts degree in School Administration from the University of Scranton.

Ray began his career as a math teacher. He taught for seventeen years in the Binghamton School District, and spent eleven years as an Associate Principal at Binghamton High School. In 1975, Ray founded Dine-A-Mate, Inc. The Dine-A-Mate coupon book was used nationwide as a fundraiser for thousands of schools and non-profit groups. Until the sale of the company in 1996, Ray led the company as CEO for more than twenty years. For four consecutive years in the early to mid-1990's, *Inc. 500* magazine recognized Dine A-Mate as one of the fastest-growing companies in America.

Ray was inducted into the Minor-Professional Football Hall of Fame in 1983. He's received numerous business and civic awards, including the Broome County Chamber of Commerce Business Person of the Year Award, and the American Legion Post 80 Person of the Year Award in 2002. He's a member of the Section IV Hall of Fame, and a recipient of the Distinguished Binghamton High School Graduate Award. And Ray isn't done yet. In 2003, he co-founded Enjoy the City with a few of his children. Enjoy the City is similar to the Dine-A-Mate concept. Once again, he's back at it. Says Ray, "Things go smoother the second time around, because you learn from your mistakes."

"I like to keep things simple, work as a team and have a 'whatever it takes' attitude. I love Broome County. This area has been a wonderful place for my wife Nikki and I to raise our seven children and twenty-nine grandchildren. The education, sports, and business climate are second to none."

Did You Know:
As a teenager Ray could frequently be seen riding a horse around Binghamton's East Side.

44

Ray Stanton

faces

Diane Stento

inspiration

When we met with Diane Stento and her daughter Danielle, Diane told us that their lives took an unsettling twist some sixteen years ago, and she never thought they would have ever been challenged to the extent they have. In 1989, Danielle, then a student at the University of Buffalo, was struck by a drunk driver. Danielle survived with permanent, traumatic brain injury that necessitates around-the-clock care.

Diane says, "You can never prepare for tragedy, and you just do everything in your power to persevere, aided by a strong faith in God. You have to make choices when your life changes... you're ripped off your path and I totally depended on my spiritual direction." Although nothing can mitigate the tragedy the Stento family suffered, Diane and the rest of her family emerged from their grief with a dedication to help others.

Diane Stento has been honored on numerous occasions for founding The Danielle House on Riverside Drive in Binghamton. This home provides out-of-town families with a safe and caring place to stay while a loved one is seriously ill or injured and hospitalized in the Binghamton area. The Danielle House is a non-profit organization and a member of the National Association of Hospitality Houses. As Diane explains, "A family extended their home when we were in time of need and we can never re-pay that. Our pay back is that we found a way to help other families in need going forward."

Diane also founded the Danielle 5-K Run/Walk, in cooperation with the STOP-DWI program, to raise money and awareness about drunk driving. The presence of Diane and Danielle at the Run always inspires the community. Both projects arose from personal adversity. The spirit of faith exhibited by Diane and Danielle continues to bring solace and hope to the many lives they touch. We're grateful to them for their example of grace and strength.

We asked Diane what gave her the strength to start The Danielle House. She replied, "My belief is that it was God's plan, not mine. Ultimately, when I knew that this [The Danielle House] was to be, I had the wisdom to not stop at the first no. Then, the pieces just miraculously came together."

Did You Know:
Diane was voted the best girl dancer at Binghamton North High School in 1964.

45

Diane **Stento**

Pete Stewart

educator

"I look forward to the educational and social challenges of preparing children for the future." Those are the words of Peter M. Stewart. "We need to focus our efforts on building a solid, early foundation for learning that incorporates technology, literacy and character education," he says. Pete is the consummate school principal. He says every decision he makes is for the betterment of the students. Currently, he is the principal of Sidney Elementary School in Sidney, New York.

Pete has a very good handle on early childhood education, and his resume explains why. He was born and raised in New York City, and attended school in the Bronx public school system before continuing his education in college. Pete earned his B.A. from SUNY Purchase, his M.S.Ed in Special Education from the College of New Rochelle, and his C.A.S. in Educational Administration from SUNY Cortland.

After his studies, he returned home and began his career as an elementary school teacher in one of the poorest schools of New York – District 7 in the Bronx. Once Pete and his wife Julie were ready to start a family, they moved to Julie's hometown of Binghamton. Pete taught for five years at MacArthur Elementary School in Binghamton before accepting his current position in Sidney.

Pete loves this area, as he explains: "I met my wife in college and during our trips to visit family I fell in love with Binghamton. When we started our own family, we decided to move to the Southern Tier because of its safe communities, its natural scenic beauty, and its excellent schools. The Southern Tier has a rich history and is truly a wonderful place to raise children."

Peter has adopted a motto for Sidney Elementary School called "The Five Pillars of Character Education: Respect / Trustworthiness / Fairness / Caring / Responsibility." He says it's very important that children learn these behavioral traits from an early age. He adds, "Kids need to develop the intrinsic motivation related to these traits." With four children of his own, Pete has a philosophy that sums up his educational goals. He states, "Given a nurturing and challenging learning environment, all children can learn."

Did You Know:
Pete plans on writing a best-selling book on successful weight loss.

46

Pete Stewart

Joan Trepa

educator

Joan Trepa has spent her life working to make the world a better place. Born and raised in Syracuse, she obtained a Bachelor's degree in Elementary Education with a minor in Music from the State University of New York at Potsdam. Her teaching career included positions at public and private schools in Maryland and New York.

Joan and her late husband, Dr. John R. Trepa, adopted five children as infants. Those children grew up to give her many grandchildren. When her children were young Joan devoted her time to the family. For fifteen years, she taught piano to students at her home, maintaining a rewarding contact with youth and providing a positive influence in their lives.

When her own children became adults, Joan returned to teaching, spending fourteen years with kindergarten and first grade students. Over the years, she has also been an active member of her community and church. Today, she volunteers as a driver for the Christian Caring Service in Greene. She also volunteers for the crisis hotline sponsored by Catholic Charities in Chenango County. To balance her life, she leads a local Red Hat group, keeping her spirit young with friends and fun.

Joan is currently writing a children's book featuring a bear that was part of her clssroom over the years. She is also writing a second book about her daughter's triumphs in living with cerebral palsy.

Joan says that she enjoys life in the Southern Tier. She gives credit for her optimistic outlook to her family, her friends, and the quality of life provided by a small American community. As she puts it, "I love the people and opportunities in this area. Who could ask for more?"

Did You Know:
Joan reads up to five books per week.

47

Joan Trepa

Mike Wales

woodworker

Michael Wales is extremely passionate about nature, and especially passionate about trees. That passion pours out into his remarkable talent as a woodworker.

He was born and raised in Norwich. He says that he was the only baby in the nursery at that time, and therefore received all of the nurses' attention. He says this may have contributed to his personality and creativity. Mike lived in Norwich until he was 10 years old. His family then moved to the Endicott area.

His passion is building "one-of-a-kind" woodworkings – everything from bed frames, to staircases, to flooring. He often will complement the piece with intricate, inlaid astrological signs. He says he gets his talent from his father and grandfather, and his inspiration from the trees themselves. "I frequently go out into the woods and actually get energy from the trees," explains Mike. One of his favorite places of serenity is Hammond Hill State Forest, which is located between Newark Valley and Ithaca. As he describes it, "There are two outrageous cherry trees at Hammond Hill which I refer to as 'sister trees' because they are only ten feet apart. I like to go there and absorb the energy they transmit. Trees give off so much energy, it's amazing, and it's something that we all can use."

Prior to owning his own business, Mike worked at a lumberyard for six years and in a production shop for nearly eight years. Mike has enjoyed being his own boss for the past fifteen years. His work is in such high demand that his waiting list extends for nearly a year. He resides in Newark Valley with his wife Debbie, their three children, three grandchildren, and five rescued greyhounds. His son, Miles, works alongside him, ensuring that this truly amazing talent will continue on.

"I think my purpose here on earth is to display the reverence of how important trees are to our being," says Mike. His creations will certainly leave behind a true and beautiful legacy.

Did You Know:
Mike enjoys watching meteor showers.

48

Mike Wales

Jackie Westcott

art teacher

When Jackie Triffo was fifteen years old and a sophomore at Binghamton Central High School, she enjoyed her art class, which was taught by Miss Ann Greiner. What she didn't know at the time was that Miss Greiner would change her life forever. During one normal school day, Jackie left a watercolor painting she had completed at the workstation in the back of the classroom. The next day, Miss Greiner opened class by holding up the painting and asking the creator to claim it. Jackie remembers being afraid to raise her hand, thinking she would be scolded for leaving her work out. Much to the contrary, Miss Greiner raved about the painting and asked Jackie to stay after class to talk. She told Jackie she saw true talent in her work, and that she should consider going into art as a career. As Jackie recalls, "This opened the door to something I never imagined. Until then, I thought I would become a nurse or something more practical."

In 1977, Jackie received a Bachelor of Fine Arts degree from the Rochester Institute of Technology, with a major in Communication Design. Jackie and her husband, John, moved to Chicago in 1977, and returned to Binghamton in 1979. She worked in the local graphics industry, first at Union Press and then at GAF. During this time, she also took classes with the noted artist, Paul Elliot. Eventually, Jackie was hired as his assistant, thus adding a new dimension to her artistic life. By 1982, she had gained the knowledge and experience to open her own art school, and her teaching career has continued over the past twenty-three years.

Jackie's years of offering art instruction have made it possible for her to reach hundreds of students with guidance and encouragement, emphasizing individual learning and technical improvement. Some of her students have gone on to professional careers in the arts, and many have been recognized for exceptional talent, with their work represented in nationally prestigious galleries. Many of her students have developed long lasting relationships with Jackie, even after their art instructions had ended. One of Jackie's former students, Danielle, says this in a recent letter to Jackie. "Jackie, your class has shaped the choices I have made in my life throughout the time I have been here. Not only have I grown as an art student past the point I thought I ever could, I have also grown and matured to be a young woman with a greater understanding of life."

An avid collector of fine art, Jackie has been able to acquire pieces by many regional artists - a collection that complements her enjoyment of life in the Binghamton area. As she puts it, "I love living in Broome County - its beauty, security, and the friendliness of the residents. And I'm very optimistic regarding the 'Arts Renaissance' now developing in downtown Binghamton. I believe it is a tribute to the amazing talent of our local artists. The success of the First Friday Gallery Walks is just the beginning of a new future for the arts in Broome County."

Did You Know:
Jackie likes to play the bongos.

49

Jackie Westcott

Kristina Wong

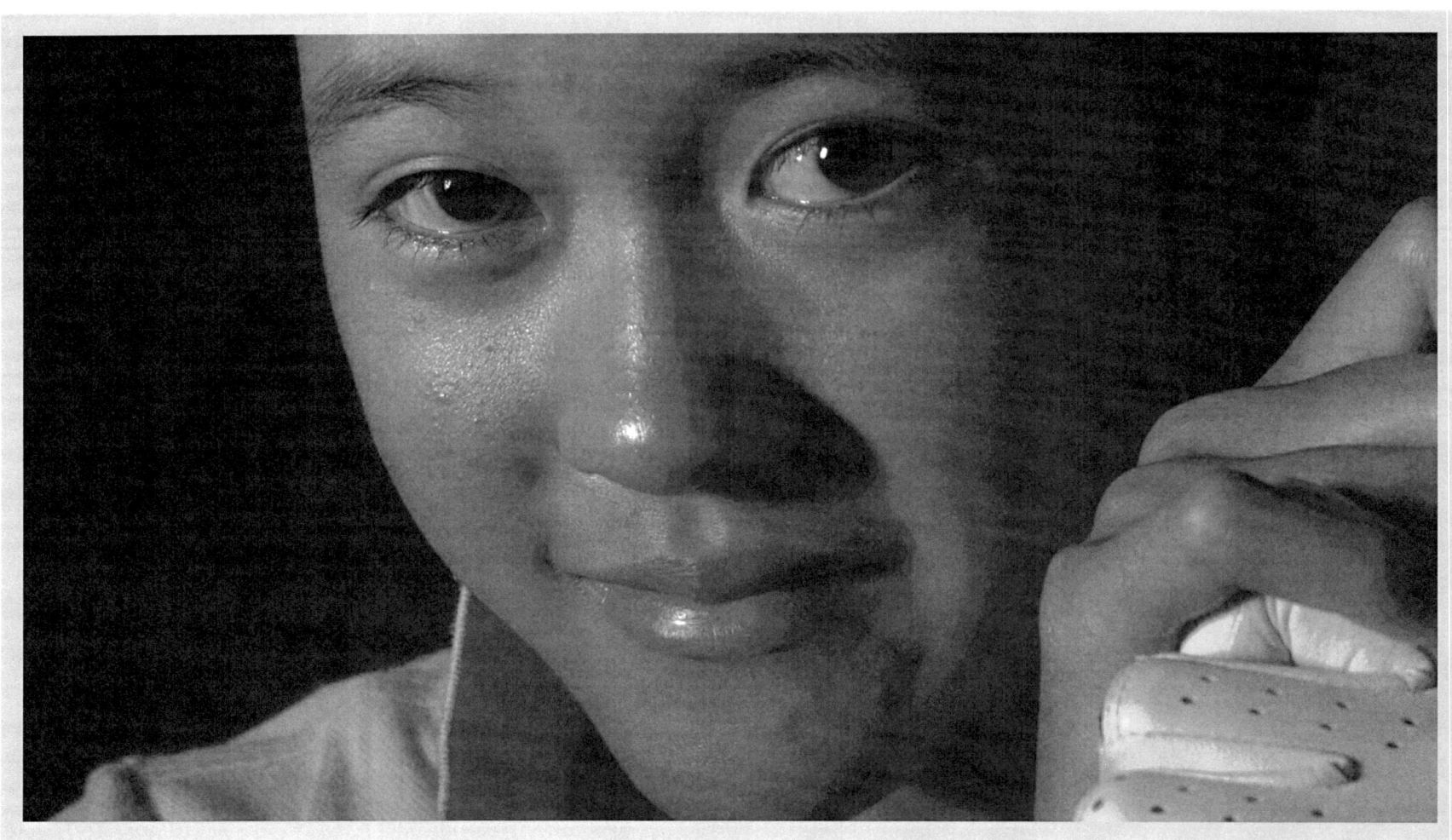

golfer

"Golf is not as boring as it seems on television. It's actually a lot of fun once you learn to hit the ball." That's how Kristina Wong describes her favorite sport.

At the age of eight, Kristina's life was changed, when her father took her to a driving range. Since that time, she has seldom put down her golf clubs. Now, at the age of fourteen, she is enrolled at the David Leadbetter Golf Academy, a special school in Florida where her talent is being honed. Regular school classes are taught in the mornings, with the afternoons given over to the mastery of golf. It is a very competitive educational facility, and ten of the top fifty young people in American golf attend school there.

Kristina has been winning golf awards since 2001, when she was a member of the First Team All-American Plantation Tour. She reappeared as a First Team All-American in 2004 and 2005. Other awards she has garnered include: the U.S. Kids Golf Championship in 2003, the Year End Championship in 2002 and 2003, and the Pepsi Little People's Golf Championship Sportsmanship Award in 2002. Kristina also qualified for the 2004 U.S. Jr. Girls Championship, and was ranked in the top 64 competitors. In 2005, she was in the top 32.

Kristina has also maintained high achievements in her scholastic endeavors. Her goals for the future include playing on a college golf team and eventually playing professional golf. Otherwise, she says she is a normal teenager who enjoys movies, music and friends.

To all the other normal teenagers out there, she says, "I would advise people my age to never give up, and to have patience in whatever is their main focus."

Did You Know:
Kristina always wears her lucky bracelet when competing in a golf tournament.

50

Kristina **Wong**

faces

Behind the Scenes

What a pleasure it was to put the first edition of *FACES* together. Our team was able to meet so many fascinating people with dynamic talents and personalities. We exchanged many stories with the subjects and had many, many laughs. We want to share some photos with you of what it was like "behind the scenes". The project took exactly 90-days to complete. We were on a tight schedule, but all the subjects were very accommodating with their time.

Enjoy the photos!

FACES of the Southern Tier - STAFF

Behind the Scenes

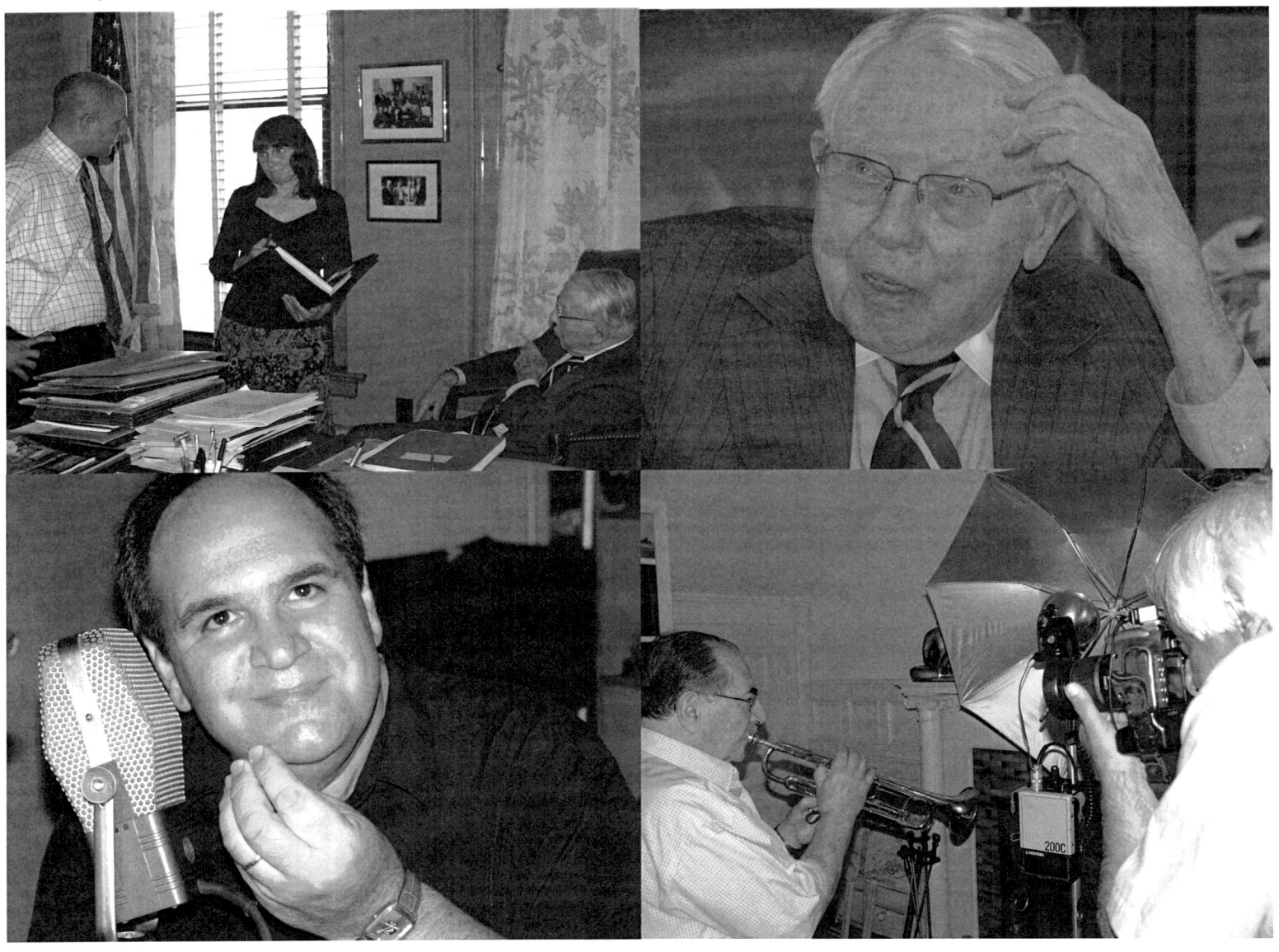

faces

Behind the Scenes

Behind the Scenes

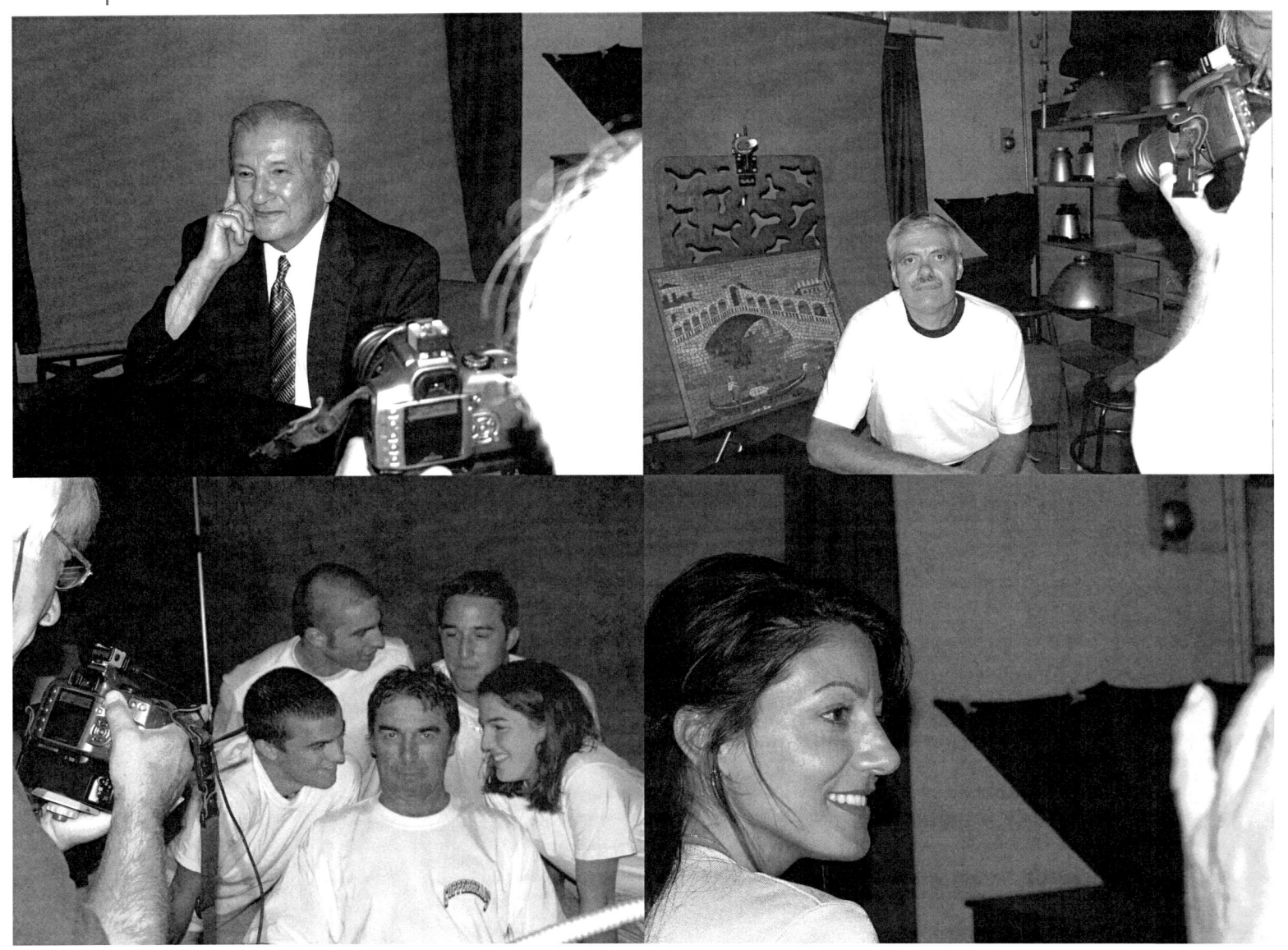

faces

Behind the Scenes

About the Authors

ROGER L. BROOKS

Roger L. Brooks, 35, is the founder of FACES Publications, LLC. He embarked on this venture in the spring of 2005 and partnered with award-winning photographer Ed Aswad and award-winning writer Suzanne M. Meredith for the first edition, *FACES of the Southern Tier*. Roger plans to produce the publication annually in the Southern Tier, as well as expand the concept beyond the local area.

Roger was born and raised in Binghamton. He attended Binghamton High School and Broome Community College before transferring to Portland State University, in Portland, Oregon in 1990. While in college, he started a t-shirt company, RIP City T's, and produced clothing for retailers throughout the Pacific Northwest.

In Portland, Roger partnered with NBA legend Clyde Drexler and in 1992 formed Slamma Jamma Sports, which produced a product line of apparel for Mr. Drexler. From 1993 – 1999, Roger joined Binghamton-based Dine-A-Mate, Inc. where he was responsible for bringing the Dine-A-Mate product to the West Coast. He played a key role in the expansion of Dine-A-Mate, which was listed in *Inc. Magazine* as one of the fastest growing private companies in America from 1994-1997. He returned to Binghamton in 1996 to work at the company's corporate office. In 2000, Roger founded Global Membership Solutions, Inc. where he is currently the Chairman and CEO.

Roger is involved with multiple business ventures and serves the community on various boards including the Zoning Board of Appeals for the City of Binghamton, the Binghamton Boys and Girls Club Foundation, and the Binghamton Zoo at Ross Park. He resides in Binghamton with his wife, Sabrina, and their daughter, Alexis.

ED ASWAD

Ed Aswad received his first camera at the age of ten years old by winning a contest for selling newspaper subscriptions. This simple box camera stimulated a lifelong passion for photography.

Ed has worked for more than 50 years as a professional photographer, and describes his career as "a cake walk through life." He received photographic training in the United States Army and was commended for bravery and dedication while recording fire fighters on a burning ship. From there, Ed returned to work in Broome County as an industrial photographer at General Electric in Johnson City. In 1969, he became a partner in Carriage House Photography, and in 1979, became the sole owner. His reputation has expanded to become the premier aerial and commercial photographer in the Southern Tier.

During his years behind the camera, Ed has recorded the changing landscape of Broome County and photographed hundreds of world known dignitaries, including three presidents of the United States.

Ed has received a Star on Binghamton's Sidewalk of Fame. He has also been given the Jefferson Award (with Suzanne Meredith) for producing books on local history. He has authored a book for children, *A Cat Tale in Spiceville*, and has dedicated a significant part of his time to the betterment of Broome County.

About the Authors

SUZANNE M. MEREDITH

Suzanne Meredith has been capturing images with words for many years, but during the past two decades her publishing record has increased phenomenally. As an author, historian and journalist, juggling words has become a profession. She is the author and/or co-author of 13 books, with publishing contracts for several more volumes that are now in progress.

Suzanne has received the Jefferson Award (with Ed Aswad) for exceptional service in the preservation and promotion of local history through the writing of photo/history books. Over the years, Suzanne has produced hundreds of magazine and newspaper articles that have been printed in numerous prestigious publications. She is currently Town of Union Historian, a position she has held for ten years, and is a correspondent for the Gannett newspaper, the Binghamton Press & Sun Bulletin.

Her accomplishments include the following:
"Tier Perceptions" staff columnist where she wrote hundreds of articles; "Checchino", A Father Son Journey Toward Dusk", by Francis Battisti with S.Meredith; Union - S. Meredith; Binghamton - E. Aswad & S. Meredith; Broome County in Vintage Postcards - Suzanne Meredith & Ed Aswad; Broome County 1859 to 1950 - E. Aswad & S. Meredith; Endicott-Johnhson Corporation - E. Aswad & S. Meredith; Footsteps in Kindness - S. Meredith & Jack Van Gorden; Gravely Interesting - Suzanne Meredith written as a fund raising project for the Association of Public Historians; House Proud - Robert Keller & Suzanne Meredith; Broome County Images - wrote half the book detailing commercial ventures in Broome County, for the Broome County Chamber of Commerce; 1001 Trivia Q & A about Broome County - Authored by Ed Aswad and Suzanne Meredith; Town of Union Civil War Enrollment & Troop Records, published by Heritage Books - Suzanne Meredith; Correspondent for Binghamton Press & Sun Bulletin - Gannett Newspapers.

Through the Lens of a Photographer

A few months ago, Roger Brooks asked if I would participate as the photographer for a project called *Faces*. After listening to his concept for this book, I recalled that just two weeks previously I had purchased a book from an old friend. The name of this volume is *Portraits Of Greatness by Yousuf Karsh*. The photographer, from Ottawa, Canada, was famous throughout the world. I greatly admired the talent Karsh demonstrated throughout the publication. Other photographers also were an influence. Two in particular I respected were local Press photographer Gene Swierkosz, and my North High photography teacher, Charles Konecny. I am sure their influence can be seen in my work.

The thought of photographing people of importance is a two-fold exercise. First is the opportunity to meet and converse in private with people of accomplishment and distinction. Second, a photographer must work with ease and speed in order not to disrupt the subject's schedule.

I was given the opportunity and challenge to get good photographic results from a child of five years old to people in their nineties. The results have been rewarding, and I hope these photos will be a lasting legacy to their contributions in the community.

My strategy for *Faces* was simple... move in tight to the face. The face is the road map of a person's life. By concentrating on the face, the viewer is not distracted by objects surrounding the subject. The camera I used is a digital, handheld without a tripod, and the color has been converted to black and white in PhotoShop. The world of photography is ever changing and challenging, and the age of digital cameras has provided an interesting experience... expanding the scope of capturing life through a lens.

The equipment I used had to be minimal, so I decided to use the Rembrant Lighting method. This means that there is an inverted triangle on the cheek, with one umbrella electronic flash. Using this method, the time needed to produce the portraits was at a minimum, taking no more than 15 minutes of shooting time.

To sum up the situation, it was a wonderful journey to meet so many people who have contributed so unselfishly of their time, talent and resources to our community. Each of these people will certainly be remembered by future generations in the book *Faces*. Thanks, Roger Brooks, I am happy to have been given the opportunity to participate in this memorable work.

-Ed Aswad

To receive more information on how you can get involved in *FACES*, or how you can bring *FACES* to your community, please call 607-723-0324, or visit www.tierfaces.com.